GROWING CHARACTER

99 Successful Strategies for the Elementary Classroom

DEB AUSTIN BROWN

Growing Character: 99 Successful Strategies for the Elementary Classroom
Copyright © 2003, Deb Austin Brown

For information, contact:
CHARACTER DEVELOPMENT GROUP
366 Bella Vista Drive
Boone, NC 28607

888-262-0572

info@CharacterEducation.com
www.CharacterEducation.com

Cover and text design by Sara Sanders

$19.95
ISBN-10: 1-892056-25-9
ISBN-13: 978-1-892056-25-2

Quantity Purchases
Companies, schools, professional groups, clubs, and other organizations may qualify for special terms when ordering bulk quantities of this title. For ordering information, contact the Customer Service Department of Character Development Publishing at the numbers listed above.

Dedication

This book is warmly dedicated to teachers, students, administrators, parents, and community members making the character journey.

Go forward! Each step of your journey makes the world a better place...one child at a time.

Also by Deb Austin Brown

Lessons From The Rocking Chair: Timeless Stories For Teaching Character
Lessons From The Beach Chair: Nature's Wisdom For Teaching Character

Author's Note

Life is a journey. I believe that we were meant to spend our lives growing in knowledge and growing in character. That requires a lifetime of study and practice. The lives and teachings of Jesus and Aristotle have impacted my life in, perhaps, the most powerful ways. I am grateful for their wisdom and their example.

Teachers are special people who help us chart our path. I have been fortunate to have wonderful and dedicated teachers along my way: Sister Margaret Rose, Lucy Marra, Bernadine Bess, Jane Bonner, Philip Brewster, June Santee, Bernard Schmitt, Caroline Cloer, and Jane Roberts. You have helped craft me into the teacher and person that I am today.

Along the way I have also met wise and wonderful men and women who have helped me grow in the character wisdom: William Mitchell, Mike Mitchell, Phil Vincent, John Handley, Charlie Abourjilie, Helen LeGette, Tom Lickona, Hal Urban, Matt Davidson, Kevin Ryan, Ben Nesbit, David Brooks, Lynn Macan, Jerry Corley, Rich Parisi, Roger Phillips, and Tony Devine.

I believe that to whom much is given, much is expected. It's ageless wisdom. I have been blessed with life experiences that have brought me insight and understanding of the character message, and I believe that it is my responsibility to pass it on. It is my hope that the wisdom found within the pages of this book will inspire and motivate you—and move you to action. The future of each child and the future of our world depend on it!

Deb Austin Brown

"Deb Brown is a fantastic teacher, a great storyteller, and a wonderful writer. She's also one of the real pioneers in character education—she's been successfully practicing it for years. Now she shares her warmth, wisdom, and practical strategies with others. They're sure to enhance the lives of teachers, parents, and kids. What a valuable resource!"

Hal Urban
Author, *Life's Greatest Lessons*
Redwood City, California

"Deb Brown is a phenomenal teacher. Like all the great ones, Deb's success begins with her heart and love for children. She calls it the character message, but it is really love and hope for the children whose lives she shares. In this wonderful work, Deb shares her stories and strategies for enveloping children in that same love and hope, at the same time giving us as teachers hope for the children in our own classrooms."

Charlie Abourjilie
High School Teacher and Coach, Author
Greensboro, North Carolina

"From the first day I entered Deb Brown's classroom as a pre-service teacher, I could sense the character message woven into all that she does with kids. Deb's exemplary teaching skills and her passion for character education have been a source of inspiration to me as she helped me to grow as a teacher and a person."

Johnny Ferrara
Teacher, Chandler Elementary School
Charleston, West Virginia

"Teaching good values and good citizenship should be a goal in every classroom today. I firmly believe the strategies used in this book will be very beneficial to all classroom teachers."

Kay F. Lee
Principal, Dunbar Primary School
Dunbar, West Virginia

"Deb Austin Brown's work has proven to be an inspiration to me as a teacher and has had a large impact on my role in effectively building the character of children."

Vicky Mayor
Teacher, Horry County Schools
Myrtle Beach, South Carolina

"If you are looking for a practical, exciting, and motivational book on character education, this is one you don't want to miss! Deb Austin Brown writes from her own experiences, which have touched thousands of lives. Deb strongly believes in the importance of academic excellence and character education for all students. This book is filled with actual experiences and activities which have taken place in her classroom. These ideas will work in your classroom, too!"

Rich Parisi
Principal, Wetzel Road Elementary
Liverpool, New York

"The character quotes in Deb Brown's book are great! Each day, my students add a quote to their Character Journals. The students love drawing an illustration to go with each quote. What a wonderful beginning to a day of learning through character!"

Linda D. Taylor
Teacher, Lakewood Elementary School
St. Albans, West Virginia

"With the help and wisdom of my friend, Deb Brown, I have learned to listen to my students and to capture every moment to instill goodness in all of them. What a joy it is to watch kindergarten students grow academically and grow in character as well! Ending each school day with a character sharing time provides my students time to appreciate, respect and care about their classmates."

Chris Ketterly
Teacher, Alban Elementary School
St. Albans, West Virginia

"Deb Brown has a long history of integrating important character concepts into her classroom, believing that learning to read and learning to do the right thing go hand in hand."

Jane Hoskins Roberts
Principal, Alban Elementary School
St. Albans, West Virginia

"This is the most comprehensive book on character development available and by a teacher who knows first-hand how to build character in students. A gold mine of ideas, resources, and how-to's!"

Michael A. Mitchell
Executive Director
Power of Positive Students Foundation
Myrtle Beach, South Carolina

Table of Contents

Introduction ix

Part 1: THE STORY 1
The Character Journey 2
Chapter One: CULTIVATING CHARACTER 3
Chapter Two: THE POWER OF ONE 11
Chapter Three: WORDS AND WISDOM 15
Chapter Four: THE CHARACTER MESSAGE 21
Chapter Five: WEAVING THE FABRIC 25
Chapter Six: GROWING IN GOODNESS 31
The Impact of Teaching for Character: A Kid Story 38

Part 2: THE STRATEGIES 39
Character in the Classroom 40
Chapter Seven: BUILDING CLIMATE 41
Chapter Eight: BUILDING CURRICULUM 79

Part 3: THE SUPPORT 109
Character Messages 110
Quotes 142
What the Kids Say 165

As We Were Going to Press 167
Afterword 169
About the Author 170

Introduction

When I travel across America to speak about the importance of teaching character, I am careful about how I introduce myself. I always preface my talks with the explanation that I am *not* an expert in the field. I am a scholar and practitioner. I am a scholar in that I read and study everything that I can get my hands on about the subject of character education and I hang out with the brilliant thinkers of our time. I wear out their doorsteps and I listen to their words. I have learned so much. I am a practitioner in that every day I roll up my shirtsleeves and go to work in the classroom with real kids.

I have been fortunate to learn and grow because of information and opportunities in the field. But I will have to say that I learned the most about character education by actually *trying* it. I teach character to my class of sixth grade students, teach a Character Class to the students in my Pre-K through sixth grade elementary school, plan and conduct monthly Character Assemblies at our school, serve as Team Leader of our school's character education initiative, teach a graduate class in character education, write books and journal articles on character development, and travel the country working with schools to further their character initiatives. Let me say that I have received more than I have given.

But I'll have to be honest. My journey on the road to implementing character education in my classroom and school hasn't always been easy. At times it's been rough and unyielding. I have run into bumps, potholes, and detours on the road. At times I have even stalled, broken down, and lost my way. On the upside, I have witnessed many scenic wonders. And in my travels, I have met talented and dedicated professionals who have given me the wisdom and strength to continue on with my journey. But, perhaps the greatest joy and learning of all has come from the students I have met and taught along the way.

Reading books, attending seminars and conferences, visiting schools, and conducting dialogue and discussions with learned professionals are all wonderful ways to learn. But the lessons that have made the greatest impact on my life are the daily lessons taught by and learned from...kids! Each year in the classroom has been different. And each year has moved me further along in my own journey to learning and living the character message. For that wisdom and understanding, I will always be grateful.

If you are *teaching* kids more than you are *learning* from them, you are missing out on so much knowledge and wisdom. My message to you is this: Tune in to their incredible insights and let the kids teach you what it is that you need to know. I believe that there is goodness and greatness in all children. And I believe that kids are naturally drawn to that goodness—and to the character message. If you are careful to listen to kids, you will learn much of what you need to know in order to help them with their own journeys to personal and academic excellence. It is this hands-on learning that will help you the most in your work with students.

This book is a travelogue of my own journey with kids. There are road signs, travel tips, sight-seeing suggestions, directions, mileage charts, and road maps all crammed inside. Within these pages are the wonderful character lessons that I have learned from working with students. It is my hope that these lessons will touch your life and warm your heart. It is my hope, too, that the wisdom herein will light the pathway of your own journey. Call each of your students to personal and academic excellence with the character message. You'll be glad that you did!

Deb Austin Brown

PART 1

The Story

The Character Journey

I've been teaching children for twenty-six years. Thinking back to my first year as a teacher, I can still remember the excitement of going to work each day, my passion for the profession and my love for my students.

These years later, nothing has changed in the Enthusiasm Department. I am still very passionate about my work. As the *Washington Post* publisher Katharine Graham once said, "To love what you do and feel that it matters, how could *anything* be more fun?" That's how I feel about my job as a teacher.

Teaching is a calling. In fact, I believe it is the highest calling. I believe that the job of a teacher is to call his or her students to personal as well as academic excellence. Students will never know how high their potential in life is unless we call them to it. It is our job and it is our duty.

Over my career I have taught thousands of lessons to my students. The wonderful thing is that my students have taught me just as much. My first teaching assignment was in a private school and I have been a character educator from the very beginning. Teaching children to be both smart and good was the expectation of that school. After ten years of teaching in three different private schools, I moved on to carry the character message into public schools.

There is simply no way to chart for you, here, my entire journey as a teacher of both academics and character. But what I can do is paint a picture for you of five special years—my last two years at Lakewood Elementary as a kindergarten teacher and my first three years at Weimer Elementary teaching sixth grade. I call this period of my life "one extreme and the other." This five-year stretch was a powerful catalyst in my growth and development as a teacher of character. It is from this time in my career, perhaps, that I learned the most.

Come with me as I chart my recent character journey. Putting one foot in front of the other, let's walk off into what could be *your* future!

Chapter One

Cultivating Character

The Character Habit

In a small-town elementary school nestled in the beautiful mountains of West Virginia, a kindergarten teacher met her new class of students. It was an unusual group for this middle-income neighborhood. Ninety percent of the students were from broken homes, forty percent had never met their birth fathers, sixty percent lived with their mothers and their current boyfriends, fifty percent lived with parents who were unemployed, and seventy percent qualified for free or reduced lunches. Even more startling was the fact that ten percent of these students had a parent who was in prison for a capital crime. The first weeks of school showed this veteran teacher that eighty percent of the students had another problem...their behavior!

I am that kindergarten teacher. And, fortunately for me and for my students, I am also a character teacher. The first month of school with this group of students was the most difficult of my twenty-one-year teaching career. At first, I was so overwhelmed I had no idea where to begin.

Picture it. The first day of school. After weeks of hard work preparing for my students, the classroom was bright, colorful, and cheerful. It was an inviting and creative environment filled with learning centers and fun activities designed to spark exploration and discovery. Surveying my masterpiece, I remember thinking that everything looked and felt just right. Then, the students arrived. An hour later, as I surveyed the room in dismay, everything looked and felt terribly wrong.

> "Moral education is not a new idea. It is, in fact, as old as education itself. Down through history, in countries all over the world, education has had two great goals: to help young people become smart and to help them become good."
>
> —**Dr. Thomas Lickona**

The children were out of control. They were not being respectful of their teacher or their classroom. Within minutes, everything was a mess! When our kindergarten transition teacher, Connie, showed up at my door, it was a great relief. She was there to help with the students who had had a difficult time the year before in our preschool program. But I couldn't help but think that divine intervention had sent her to help me! At the end of her scheduled hour in my room, I grabbed her arm and begged her not to go. Giving it my best shot, I said, "Connie, p-l-e-a-s-e don't leave. Don't leave me here alone with these kids!" Connie did leave me to face the rest of the day alone.

At the end of the day, I drove wearily home to the solitude and solace of my home. Discouraged and worried about the year ahead, I poured myself a glass of iced tea, popped in a lemon wedge and went outside to sit on the deck. Then I buried my head in my hands...and cried.

I thought, *Well, Deb, this is it! It has finally happened. You have lost your touch. You can no longer manage the students. It's time to get out of teaching and let the younger, more capable teachers take over.*

That first day had been so difficult, I was seriously considering retirement. Then I thought back to the movie *Babe*, and was reminded of a wonderful line: "Farmer Hoggett knew that the little ideas that tickled, nudged and refused to go away must not be ignored. They are the seeds of destiny."

> "Farmer Hoggett knew that the little ideas that tickled, nudged and refused to go away must not be ignored. They are the seeds of destiny."

As I thought of that quote, I remembered my studies in character education. Then it dawned on me that there was a reason I had trained in that area, and now that reason was staring me in the face! Before I could begin teaching academics to my students, I had to give them the foundation for all learning—the character message. And that's where we began our journey.

Searching for a way to begin using character principles to help my students, I thought back to my own childhood. Many of the great character lessons I learned came at the knee of a caring adult, my great-grandmother. She was a wonderful storyteller, who ended every childhood story with a memorable moral lesson. So many years later, I still recalled the great moral lessons of my youth. Those lessons gave me a *moral rope* to hold on to during the decision times of childhood...and beyond. So, in my class I tried to replicate those lessons, challenging my students to learn *the character message* from every story. I taught them that all of us are responsible for carving out our own character through the decisions we make and the habits we develop. As we began saying in our class, "Get the character habit!"

Using the traits of good character as the focus for all that I did, I tried to help my students establish good attitudes, habits, goal setting, and a work ethic that would contribute to the development of their true potential. It was a difficult task at first, but with determination and patience, we ended up having a wonderful year, despite that difficult first day. One of the principles that helped transform that class was my belief that there is *goodness* and *greatness* in every student. And, I believe that a foundation of good habits and a solid work ethic will transcend the classroom to *every* area of a child's life. What a wonderful thing it is when the child's good *work ethic* becomes his good *life ethic*!

From Work Ethic to Life Ethic

Teaching for character translates academically. That is a powerful lesson teachers, parents, and students alike need to learn. Teachers who embrace that lesson can make a wonderful difference with their students! Two of the best lessons for ensuring academic success are related to habits and work ethic.

Habits are powerful in defining one's life and charting one's destiny. Research conducted at both Harvard and Stanford universities shows that between ninety and ninety-five percent of a typical person's daily activities are the product of habit. That powerful statistic demonstrates how much of our life is chained to old behaviors that may have begun as innocent, spontaneous decisions. So many people end up learning this powerful truth about habits the hard way. But there is always a choice. A person can consciously choose to develop good habits that will serve as the foundation for a successful life, or alternately to acquire bad habits that become difficult and time consuming to break. For this reason, teachers should continually look at the classroom habits they are choosing for themselves and their students.

Developing a good work ethic is another important focus for character education in the classroom. For this area, literature is a wonderful teacher. *The Three Little Pigs* offers a memorable lesson on the importance of doing a job well. *The Little Red Hen* demonstrates how those who work hard enjoy the fruits of their labor. *The Little Engine That Could* showcases the importance of confidence, determination, and perseverance. That book was especially popular in my kindergarten class, where "I'll try!" became the class motto. The lesson from that story helped students develop the needed confidence and determination to get any job done. In that classroom, and the others that followed, the moral lessons of good literature played an instrumental role in weaving the character message throughout every activity!

In the spring, while working on a unit of study on wind and storms, we were constructing a Venn Diagram on the constructive and destructive characteristics of wind. Like a bolt out of the blue, one student said, "Gee, that's just like character! There are good and bad habits that either make the pillars stronger or tear them down." That was a stunning moment and evidence the character lessons were working.

Constructive Habits Build Up Character

Helping others
Staying on task
Telling the truth
Showing respect
Being fair
Being honest
Following rules
Being responsible
Showing kindness
Doing the right thing
Having a good work ethic

Destructive Habits Tear Down Character

Calling people names
Breaking rules
Being irresponsible
Hurting others
Being selfish
Getting even
Being lazy
Giving up
Telling lies
Not trying our best
Taking things that belong to others

I quickly grabbed the chart paper, encouraged all of the students to share their thoughts, and began recording their observations. From what they said, it was obvious they understood that good habits build up character and bad habits tear it down. As we listed bad habits on the chart, one student, Donnovan, even remarked that he could hear the pillar of character cracking and starting to break! Later, when the new character charts were displayed in the classroom, the *bad habits pillar* was drawn with a crack in the foundation. This became a wonderful visual aid, one that students often referred to the rest of the school year. In fact, whenever a student was seen breaking a rule, another classmate would say, "Oh, no! I think I hear the character pillar breaking again!"

The Power of Setting Goals

Learning to set goals seemed like the logical next step. While volunteering at The Power of Positive Students International Foundation over many years during the summers, I learned a lot about the power of goal setting. Dr. William Mitchell, a renowned educator and writer, shared the research with me.

The research findings were startling! Now I understood why my grandmother had so often advised me to write down my goals. I remember a time when I was about nine years old. My grandmother, Nina, had asked me about my plans for the future. I told her that I wanted to write a book. She responded with this wise directive: "Write it down. Write down your goal." She said that would keep me focused. My grandmother was right! And these many years later, here was Dr. Mitchell sharing the same fundamental wisdom.

Perhaps the most famous study on the importance of goals was conducted by Yale University on the school's 1953 graduating class. Granted this is old research, but the findings were riveting. The students were each given a survey that asked the following three questions related to goals. The questions were:

87%	**Do not have goals**
10%	**Have goals**
3%	**Have written goals**

Those who write down their goals achieve 50 to 100 times more than those who do not write down their goals!

Be a member of the 3% Club!

1. **Have you set goals?**
2. **Have you written them down?**
3. **Do you have a plan to accomplish them?**

Only three percent responded "yes" to all three questions. Twenty years later, in 1973, surviving members of the Class of '53 were surveyed again. The three percent who had said yes to all three questions in 1953:

> • **Were happier with their marriages**
> • **Had a better family life**
> • **Were more successful**
> • **Enjoyed better health**

Yes!

Also, the three percent who said yes owned 97 percent of the net worth of the Class of '53.

Using that powerful research as a basis for goal-setting sessions in my classroom, I taught my students to become reflective about what that they wanted to do with their lives. These kindergarten students had goals that included learning to read, having more friends, getting along better with their classmates, being better at sports, making better grades on their report cards, and being *kids of character*. Even these young students were beginning to see how setting goals could take them to wonderful places! Below are examples of some the goals my students began to set.

Academic Goals	**Social Goals**	**Personal Goals**
• Do my homework	• Be nice to others	• Learn to read
• Listen to the teacher	• Share	• Do a cartwheel
• Follow the rules	• Be helpful	• Hit the ball in my teeball game
• Sit still and listen	• Take turns	• Ride my bike without training wheels
• Practice math	• Treat everyone with respect	• Score a goal in soccer
• Follow directions	• Show self-control	• Learn to draw
• Study my spelling words	• Make friends	

Our Decisions Define Us

When young students first enter a classroom, they need motivation for learning and living the character message. Often that inspiration comes in the form of extrinsic motivation, including recognition and praise for their good efforts and deeds. Children thrive on words of praise, smiles, hugs, pats on the back, and certificates of recognition. These are effective ways to reinforce the character effort. But even the youngest student needs to learn through experience the wonderful feeling that comes from doing the right thing. I always tell my students about this feeling so that they will know that intrinsic motivation is the ultimate goal for learning and living the character message. I tell them that the special thing about *the feeling* is that no one can ever take it away from them. Even though they may not understand at first, they can grasp the idea that they will experience this feeling if they do the right thing. By often referring to the internal reward, I build it up as something to which they can look forward!

I'll never forget the time that two of my students learned first hand how good it can feel when one does the right thing.

Cody and Donnovan had just returned from gym class. "Ms. Brown," Cody said, "you'll never believe what happened in gym class! Some kid in the other class broke two pillars of character!"

"Tell me about it," I said, and the boys explained that they were playing scoop ball with partners, when one of the children in another class took their ball.

"We told the teacher about it, and he lied to her," said Donnovan. "He said he didn't take it. So he broke two pillars!"

"Two pillars?" I replied.

"Yes, two pillars of character! He *stole* our ball, and then he *lied* about it!" said Cody. The boys went on to tell me that they were angry about the incident. "We felt like kicking and hitting and doing karate chops on that kid!" they said.

"What *did* you do?" I asked.

"We thought about it, and then we decided to do the right thing," said one of the boys. "We just went and got another ball—and went back to playing the game."

"I'm very proud of you!" I told them.

Cody excitedly commented, "The neat thing was...I got it!"

"Got what?" I asked.

"I got that feeling in my heart when I did the right thing!"

> "I got it! I got that feeling in my heart when I did the right thing!"
>
> —Cody, age 6

This was one of those especially rewarding moments all teachers hope for and a time for one of my good cries. As Cody's classmates gathered around, he told them the story. Watching this unfold, I just kept thinking that sometimes children are the very best teachers of all!

The Power and Promise of Educating for Character

Every day in my classroom, I saw the power and promise of educating for character. My students underwent an incredible metamorphosis that year. By February, it was becoming evident that they had not only learned the character message, but had chosen to live it as well. One unusual morning proved the point.

I had been up most of the night working on a project, so it was very late when I finally made it to bed. During the night the power was knocked out and my alarm clock did not go off. When I woke up late, I was in a panic and called the principal for classroom coverage until I could get to school. I hurriedly jumped into the shower, dressed and put my baseball cap over my wet hair and the drove the two miles to school. By the time I arrived, class had been in session for more than twenty minutes.

I arrived in my classroom to find my students alone, with no adult supervision. The principal had forgotten to send someone in to cover the class. But there, before me, was the most beautiful sight! These young students were at their tables, quietly at work. They were drawing pictures and writing in their journals. Each and every one was on task. The classroom was so quiet, you could hear the proverbial pin drop! The homework basket was filled with the previous night's assignment; student book bags and jackets were hung neatly on their hooks in the lockers. The lunch graph was completed and tallied—and attendance had been taken. I had been marked absent. The academic day had begun without me.

I dropped my briefcase in surprise and asked, "What are you doing?"

"We're doing our work," was the answer.

It was then that I asked the silliest question: "Why?"

Donnovan piped up, "Why do you look so surprised? You taught us to have a good work ethic!"

Jeff added, "Remember? We're the kids of character. We don't do what's easy...we do what's right!"

I couldn't help but smile.

I sat down on the counter by the classroom sink, took the hairdryer out of my briefcase, and began drying my hair. As I did, I watched the

> Once in a while you will get a little glimpse into the power and impact of your teaching. Cherish each of those precious moments.

miracle at work in my classroom—an entire class of kindergarten students living out the character message right before my eyes! Yes, the beginning-of-school percentages for this class may have been stacked against them. But despite the odds, one hundred percent of my young students had learned, internalized and had chosen to live by the character message! It's a day that I'll always remember...and cherish!

A Success Story
The Kindergarten Kids of Character, 1997-1998

80%	Were behavior problems at the beginning of school
90%	Were from a broken home
70%	Lived in a trailer or rental apartment
40%	Did not know the identity of their birth father
20%	Were rejected by their birth mother, who kept other siblings
50%	Saw only one parent
60%	Lived with their mother and her current boyfriend
50%	Lived with a parent who was unemployed
70%	Were on free or reduced lunch
10%	Had a parent in prison for a major crime
100%	Learned, internalized and chose to live by the character message!

Chapter Two

The Power of One

A Touching Visit

Never underestimate the power of one caring adult in the life of a child. That concern and interest can carry a child a long way in developing a life of character. One year with a teacher of character can become the catalyst for change in any student's life. Even in these complex technological times, the most important element in teaching is still the *human* element. And, just as one caring teacher can influence the life of a child, one teacher committed to the character message can influence the direction of an entire school. Sow good seeds and be a patient gardener. It takes time, but the harvest will be bountiful!

The best story of my teaching career comes from one of my students, whom I'll call Cody. Cody was a five-year-old student who entered school in the fall excited about meeting new friends and learning new things. During the first week of school, Cody told me that he lived with his mom, her new boyfriend and his two younger brothers in the nearby trailer park. "I want for you to know that my *real* dad is in prison—for murder, " he said.

I looked at Cody in surprise. Cody went on to explain, "Dad and his friends were trying to steal some stereo equipment. Dad's job was to hold the gun...but it was supposed to be empty. His friends set him up. They put real bullets in the gun. My daddy didn't know. He didn't mean to kill anyone, but it did happen."

I was shocked and saddened by Cody's story, but could see into Cody's heart and feel his pain. My heart went out to him.

> "There is no stimulus like that which comes from the consciousness of knowing that others believe in us."
>
> —**Orison Swett Marden**

"The charges were reduced to manslaughter," continued Cody, "so my dad won't have to stay in prison forever. But he will have to stay for a long, long time." As he told his story, it seemed that a *long, long time* must have felt like *forever* to this young boy.

During the first months of school, I used Cody's desire to have contact with his father as motivation for him to learn the letters of the alphabet and their sounds so that he could learn to read and write. These skills would help Cody keep in touch with his father, who was so very far away.

In December, Cody arrived at school one day with exciting news. "I get to go and visit my dad!" he announced.

"When, Cody, when?" his classmates asked.

"Over Christmas vacation!" he said. Cody was especially happy because he could visit his father in person. "We won't have to talk over the phone with the glass between us," Cody explained. "I'll really get to touch my daddy!"

When Christmas break was over, I waited by the classroom door for Cody's return. As soon as he entered the room, Cody's smile began to grow.

"Well...how was it?" I asked. "How was your visit with your dad?"

"It was wonderful!" said Cody. "I got to go in this room with my dad. And I even got to sit on his lap! We played checkers and we wrestled. And my dad even got to tickle me. Do you know how long it's been since my dad tickled me?"

Cody continued: "You know, Ms. Brown...on the way home in the car, I just kept thinking about my dad. I didn't say much to my mom during the drive home. I just kept looking out of the car window...and thinking. And, I figured out that if my dad had been in your class, that he would never have gone to prison. He would have learned about good character and he would have made better decisions with his life."

My eyes began to well with tears. A little boy, Jeff, ran over to see why his teacher was crying. A very observant student, Donnovan, explained, "There's nothing wrong with Ms. Brown, Jeff—it's just one of her *good* cries."

Yes, it was one of my *good* cries. In fact it was one of my *best* cries! This young student had just discovered the bottom line on life and had reinforced for me the importance and power of teaching the character message.

> "When you break a pillar
> of character,
> you hurt everyone."
>
> —Cody, age 6

> There is excitement, magic, power
> and promise in educating for character.
> Great promise indeed!

An Important Influence

Research and conventional wisdom tell us that the adult who spends the greatest amount of time in significant interaction with a child will have the most influence on his or her life. My experience has shown that this is true. During late November of this past sixth-grade school year, a boy named Joseph drove home the point. It was the last day of school before the Thanksgiving holiday. Our school was having its annual Thanksgiving luncheon for parents and students. The children at our school had taken home a written invitation for their parents to join us for a turkey lunch with all of the fixings.

The big day arrived. Only seven of my students had a parent or family member show up for lunch. That left eighteen students standing in the lunch line alone. I do understand that many parents have a difficult time getting off from work during the school week. I'm not trying to assess blame or assign guilt. But some of the students standing alone in that lunch line had parents who didn't work, who could have made the effort. Joseph was one of those children.

I smiled at the loners and announced that I was changing my identity. "For these next thirty minutes, I will no longer be your teacher. I will be your substitute parent," I said. "You can just call me Mom. I would love to have the wonderful privilege of eating lunch with you."

Joseph's response was painfully honest. "You might as well sit with us at lunch. You love us more than our parents do. And you spend lots more time with us than they do."

I tried hard to take that remark as the wonderful compliment that Joseph intended for it to be. But inside, my heart was breaking for him and the other students.

"I've been in school here for eight years," Joseph added. They have these lunches every year. My mom doesn't work and she never has come to have lunch with me."

Who would you think had the most influence over Joseph at this point in his life? His mother or his teacher? I felt that I did.

This is a tremendous responsibility for any teacher. But with the character message under our belts, teachers have the tools to live up to that awesome challenge. We can lead by positive example. We have the ability to help all of our students grow in knowledge, grow in character and grow in goodness.

There is a very positive success story to share about Joseph. When he started his sixth-grade year in my classroom, Joseph was low on confidence. He had a long track record of low grades and poor behavior. Yes, we had a few tough and tense moments in the classroom during that first month of school. Joseph tried me and tested me in every way. I even had to suspend him—twice. But during that initial trial period, Joseph began to see the light. He figured out that I loved him and cared about him and was going to hold him to a high standard—the character standard. He came aboard!

Joseph went on to earn a spot on the B Honor Roll for the first nine-week grading period and earned that same spot for the second and third nine weeks, as well. But something happened during the last nine weeks of school, and Joseph's name was not on that list. Why? Joseph had worked his way to the top of the list and made the *A Honor Roll*! The character message had worked!

Joseph is now a firm believer. He knows that achieving academic success is hard work, and he chooses to do it anyway. In fact, there is one more bit of good news before this story ends. At the end of the school year, Joseph earned a *Presidential Award for Educational Improvement*. It was, in fact, his proudest moment. No, Joseph's mother was not in attendance at the Awards Banquet when Joseph was presented with his pin and certificate. But our entire staff was! And so were his proud and cheering classmates. None of us would have missed it for the world. I believe that Joseph felt the same way!

Reflecting on the wonderful changes that have taken place in Joseph's and Cody's lives, I think about all of the character seeds that I have planted with my students. Sometimes teachers are around when those seeds begin to grow and bloom. Sometimes it doesn't happen until years later and we aren't able to witness the wonderful event. Unfortunately, there *are* seeds that we plant that never quite take root.

In Joseph's case, the effort was successful. All of us at Weimer School worked hard to help him cultivate his garden. As his teacher, I planted plenty of seeds. Joseph worked hard to water the seeds and to pull the weeds. He also let the light of the character message shine on his garden. Thankfully, there was a bountiful harvest! Joseph went on to junior high school to carry on his new tradition of excellence.

Teachers need to remember that we are not planting for just this one growing season. We are planting for life! Like perennials, these blooms can return year after year. As the master gardeners, teachers need to give their students the tools to help keep their gardens healthy and thriving. Hard work, determination, perseverance, effort, honesty, responsibility, and integrity all play key roles. By teaching the character message, we make those tools available to each of our students. By choosing to live out the character message, your students can harvest beautiful, healthy gardens of their own.

Chapter Three

Words and Wisdom

The Power of Words

John Dewey, William James, and Dale Carnegie have all taught us that the deepest need in human nature is to be noticed, appreciated, and affirmed. In every classroom today are the undiscovered Einsteins, Lincolns, Edisons, and Mother Teresas of tomorrow. It is our job as teachers to believe in our students until our students can believe in themselves. By taking a child under your wing and showing sincere interest and caring, you can help chart his character growth in powerful ways! The words of Cavett Robert can serve as a powerful reminder: "Three billion people on the face of the earth go to bed hungry every night. But four billion people go to bed hungry every night for a simple word of encouragement and recognition." A teacher's words of encouragement and instruction can be powerful tools in the character development of his or her students.

Many years ago, a talented kindergarten teacher, whom I will call Nancy, showed me this wonderful analogy about the power of words. Her story paints an unforgettable picture.

A child's self-concept is as fragile as a piece of paper. When a parent fusses at breakfast, "Katey, you're always playing around with your cereal. You're making yourself late for school every day. Aren't you tired of being late for school? Just look at you! You haven't even brushed your hair yet! Hurry up! Can't you do anything right?"

"As one afflicted with feelings of inferiority and poor self-esteem as a youth, I am particularly sensitive to the importance of caring, love, encouragement, and praise from those whose lives touch mine. Encouragement and praise growing out of love and caring have the power to change a life, and that life may in turn change others."

—**Dr. Norman Vincent Peale**

RIP! A piece of self-respect is torn from the child.

Later that day, the teacher joins in: "Katey, I've already explained the directions once. Don't you ever listen?"

RIP! Another piece of the child's self-concept is torn away.

Soon, the piece of paper is noticeably smaller in size. As confidence goes, so does her ability to meet with success. The proverbial dog begins chasing its tail. It's definitely downhill after that.

Think of your own life. Disappointments often fill us with self-doubt. At times, we've all wondered if we'd ever reach any of our goals. Now, think back to a teacher who was there for you and encouraged you and offered support. He may have told you that you were a special person, with special characteristics and abilities and, in the process, helped you see the good in yourself. Because that teacher believed in you, you were able to believe in yourself. This helped you move on to tackle problems, to learn new things, to make better decisions, to gain new strides, to climb new mountains, to face the world and its challenges—and possibly even challenge the world at times.

Believing in someone carries great power, as does using a gentle, positive approach when offering instruction and correction. A favorite story from my childhood illustrates this point.

I was four years old, sitting at the kitchen table. My mother had supplied art materials and I was at work, drawing, scribbling, and writing while my mother worked alongside me in the kitchen. The phone rang and she had to leave the room. Then I ran out of paper. I knew better than to interrupt my mother, who was still on the phone. Then I noticed a clean white wall, climbed down from the kitchen chair and continued crafting my masterpiece.

A little while later, Mom returned. "Oh, no!" she said, at first clearly dismayed at the sight of her kitchen wall. But, sucking in her breath, she caught herself and took an important mental step back and smiled. Gently, lovingly, and with conviction, she said, "Deb, I can tell that you're going to be a wonderful writer. But don't write on the wall again because your dad won't like having to paint the kitchen."

That was over forty years ago, but I remember it as if it were yesterday. The vivid memory of her positive first response to my "mural" left a powerful message. Rather than criticizing or punishing me, my mother used that situation to both save her kitchen wall and empower me as a writer. That power stays with me today as I write articles, stories, presentations, and books such as this one. As teachers, we have similar opportunities every day to criticize or empower our students.

Are you an architect and builder of human potential...
or are you part of the demolition crew?

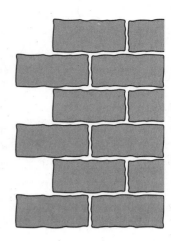

**Harsh
critical
pejorative
negative
demeaning
cutting
degrading
shaming
*words can
tear down.***

**Motivating
supportive
positive
encouraging
inspiring
expecting
reassuring
understanding
*words can
build up.***

Words Mean Something

When I started first grade in the late 1950s, I watched my teachers...really watched them. I studied their actions and listened to their words. It didn't take long to figure out how they felt about the value of a child.

As a child, one of my favorite stories was *The Little Engine That Could*. That Little Engine became my personal measuring stick for teachers. My elementary teachers either made the other students, and me, feel like that Little Engine—or they didn't. It was simple to see. The best teachers were those who were sensitive to their students, believed in them, valued them, and called them to excellence.

School year after school year, I continued to size up my teachers by that measure. If a teacher listened, responded, smiled, encouraged, praised, motivated, cheered, inspired, and looked for the best, she received high marks. If she lectured, reacted, frowned, criticized, rolled eyes in disgust, discouraged, belittled, and complained, that teacher didn't measure up to being what she could and should be. I saw that a teacher's attitude towards the students in her class determined whether they were successful or not.

Year after year, I watched how all of us responded to our teachers and began to realize that student progress often said more about the teacher than the students. Over time, it became clear that the teacher had the power to make all the difference! The teacher's attitude was the key. The sky really was the limit when a teacher's approach to student achievement was based on this perspective! I began to believe that *all* children could meet with some measure of success if they had a teacher who, like that Little Engine, really believed. It was a powerful lesson! And I knew, by that early elementary age, that I wanted to be a part of that power.

"I've come to the frightening conclusion that I am the decisive element in the classroom. It is personal approach that creates the climate. It is my daily mood that makes the weather. As a teacher, I possess a tremendous power to make a child's life miserable or joyous. I can be a tool of torture or an instrument of inspiration."

—Haim Ginott

Teachers are like mirrors. Students see themselves in these mirrors, class after class, day after day, school year after school year. That is why it is important that a teacher's "mirror" reflect each child in a positive way. In his bestseller, *The 7 Habits of Highly Effective People*, Stephen Covey said it well: "*Being* is *seeing* in the human dimension. And what we *see* is highly interrelated to what we *are*." As a mirror it is essential, then, to reflect a positive belief in each student. That feeling of being valued and having someone to believe in him will carry a student a long way on his journey to personal and academic excellence. A student's success in school—and his success later in life—depends on it! "Whether you think you can or think you can't, you're always right!" said Henry Ford. He, too, knew the powerful lesson of that Little Engine.

Mike Mitchell, Executive Director of The Power of Positive Students International Foundation in Myrtle Beach, South Carolina, and I have discussed the value of positive comments to kids. He said it well. "Words mean something." Words have the power to change a life in positive ways. They can chart a destiny. But they also have the power to destroy a life. Be careful, and choose your words wisely. The lives of your students may very well depend on it.

The Power of Truth

According to Ralph Waldo Emerson, our main want and need in life is someone who will inspire us to be what we know we can be. Dan Rather took Emerson's idea a step further when he wrote, "The dream begins with a teacher who believes in you, who tugs and pushes and leads you to the next plateau, sometimes poking you with a sharp stick called *truth*."

> "The dream begins with a teacher who believes in you, who tugs and pushes and leads you to the next plateau, sometimes poking you with a sharp stick called truth."
>
> —**Dan Rather**

There is promise in inspiration, great promise! I remember one very special day in my kindergarten classroom that illustrates the magic a teacher can weave when using encouragement.

The basic ingredients were all there ahead of time: self-confidence, skill development, motivation, inspiration, and opportunity. My class wrote in a journal every day. Following journals, each student would select a book for silent reading. This day was different. I told the students that they would find a book to read in their chair pockets. "These books are very special," I said. "You will be able to read them all by yourself when you touch them with the magic wand of self-confidence. If you think you will be able to read them all by yourself, you will."

Each of the twenty-three students had a different eight-page book, which they had never read before. There were only one or two sentences on each page. Most of the children tackled their books with enthusiasm. However, a few of the less confident students remained skeptical. Then, after a few minutes, one student, Lauren, jumped up excitedly, almost tripping over her feet.

"I can read it! I can read it...all by myself!" she cried. I quickly went to her. Meanwhile, the other children stopped reading, their eyes fixed intently on Lauren.

"Read it to us," I said. Lauren stood proudly beside me and read her book. When she finished, spontaneous applause broke out in the room. Inspired by Lauren's success, each child then tackled his own book. Over the next thirty minutes, they then read their books aloud to me or my kindergarten aide, Pat. As each student was done, he skipped up the hallway and surprised our principal by reading to her. Our principal ran out of stickers that day. Inspired by encouragement, those children were on a mission. This exercise in self-confidence helped them become kids of conviction, kids with courage, and kids of character!

The Power of Wisdom

I was raised on wisdom and still remember the stories and lessons that were part of my own childhood. There are many opportunities in the classroom to build character by sharing one's wisdom. An important part of teaching character comes from the many *incidental* teachable moments that arise throughout the day to share that wisdom. But *intentional* lessons can also be also taught through the use of stories, fables, fairy tales, proverbs, and real-life stories from the lives of my students. The moral lessons of these stories can be repeated at transitional times throughout the school day:

> - **Actions speak louder than words.**
> - **Honesty is the best policy.**
> - **The best way to have a friend is to be a friend.**
> - **Say what you mean and mean what you say.**
> - **Hard work never hurt anyone.**
> - **You can go a long way after you are tired.**
> - **Don't do what's easy, do what's right.**
> - **Don't try to be anyone else, just be yourself.**
> - **Our decisions define us.**
> - **Be a good-deed-doer.**
> - **Be in the right place at the right time, doing the right thing.**

and the moral is...

We repeat these messages when we're changing classes, lining up for recess, washing our hands for lunch, and packing our book bags at the end of the school day. These character-building moments take no time out of the daily schedule, yet are powerful in helping children internalize the character message. By repeating these core ideas five or six times each day, 180 days each school year, my young students commit them to memory. This gives them a *moral rope* on which to hold during the decision-making times of childhood and beyond—and helps make character a *way of life*!

This may sound like a small and insignificant habit to work on in your own classroom, yet it is one of the most important things a teacher can do to help children learn, remember, and internalize those ideas. This quote by Bruce Barton addresses this point: "Sometimes when I consider what tremendous consequences come from little things...I am tempted to think...there are no little things"

This is especially true applied to the practice of repeated wisdom.

"Sometimes when I consider what tremendous consequences come from little things...
I am tempted to think...
there are no little things."

These daily anecdotal findings support my claim:

- Walking through the cafeteria one day, I overheard two students in the lunch line trying to recall as many bits of wisdom as they could before they reached the food window.
- On the school playground, I overheard a student remind a friend who was considering hitting back after an altercation: "Don't do what's easy...do what's right!"
- During independent class work, I have heard students remind their classmates: "Hard work never hurt anyone."
- And one day after school in the gym, I heard two cheerleaders discussing whether or not to include another girl in a weekend party, when one invoked this adage: "The best way to have a friend is to be a friend."

The list, fortunately, goes on! The act of repeated wisdom is one thing that I'll never give up in my day-to-day interactions with students. It's one *little* thing that reaps *big* rewards!

Without adult guidance, children can come up with their own ideas on wise living. Over the years, as I've picked up these ideas, I've written then down. There's a saying that to steal ideas from one is plagiarism, but to steal from many is research. So, below are a few of my research findings. You may remember the original wisdom of these sayings but, as you will see, children can come up with some good ideas of their own!

Kid Wisdom

- Don't bite the hand that. . . . . *looks dirty.*
- The pen is mightier than the. *pigs.*
- Strike while the. . . . . *bug is close.*
- An idle mind is. . . . . *the best way to relax.*
- A penny saved is . . . . *not much.*
- You can't teach an old dog new . . . . *math.*
- Better be safe than . . . . *punch a fifth grader.*
- It's always darkest right before . . . . *daylight savings time.*
- Two's company, three's. . . . . *the musketeers.*
- Children should be seen and not . . . . *spanked or grounded.*
- Laugh and the world laughs with you, cry and . . . . *you have to blow your nose.*

Chapter Four

The Character Message

The Journey Toward Wisdom

Messages are all around us. Life's messengers are often disguised as parents, teachers, sages, and friends. Or they may be historians, poets, philosophers, and counselors. What these messengers have in common is a willingness to share life's lessons from the human experience. Those of us who want to learn search them out. We read, study, research, and ask. Our quest becomes a life journey toward wisdom.

> "Good character is a thing remembered."
> —Ptah-hotep, 27th century B.C.

The character message is an important one. I believe that it is our duty as teachers to deliver it to our students. It is one of the best ways to call students to personal and academic excellence, because the character message has the power to change their lives.

Real-life character messages are all around us. Creating an awareness of these natural messages is one of the greatest gifts you can give your students. Students are naturally drawn to these messages and to their memorable lessons. Character messages also draw on the innate desire in each child to gravitate to the side of goodness. Students need structure, boundaries, direction, and guidance. That important job belongs to both parents and teachers. And when the home and school join hands in the effort, the impact of character training becomes all encompassing! This consistency then becomes character training and a powerful force that can bring about major change in the life of a student.

Years ago, I met a man who would transform my life. Dr. William Mitchell had written a book called *The Power of Positive Students*. A college professor had given me a copy of the book to read. Read it, I did! Dr. Mitchell's ideas were so in tune with mine that I had to write him a letter. I mailed it to his office in Myrtle Beach, South Carolina, not knowing the impact that book and letter would later have on my life.

In response, I received a warm and wonderful letter, inviting me for a visit. I'm sure that it was no coincidence that our family had a beach house just seven miles from Dr. Mitchell's office, in Garden City Beach. I couldn't wait for my next beach trip! On November 3, 1992, I made the trip. That meeting began a new mentoring relationship and friendship that continues to sustain me. One of the many lessons Dr. Mitchell taught me was the difference between *interest* and *commitment*. Are you merely interested in teaching children the character message—or are you committed to it? It's an essential question.

In the daily classroom trenches, it's a question I often ask myself. I've found it is important to reflect about all I do with my students and question every move that I make. Teachers need to ask themselves, daily, if they are really committed to the character initiative with their students or if they view it as a casual interest. Are their character efforts with children *incidental* or are they *intentional*? Are they an *add-on* or are they *built in*? It's definitely food for thought!

> "Values are built-ins, not add-ons."
>
> **—Ben and Jerry's Double Dip**

With so many character messages already around us, it makes sense to pull lessons from nature and from life. The best character lessons are from real life. Dr. Hal Urban's incredibly insightful book, *Life's Greatest Lessons*, is packed full of them! I've read this book four times from cover to cover and still pick it up when in need of direction, motivation and a renewed dose of enthusiasm for life. The wisdom gained from just living life is perhaps the most valuable wisdom of all. Why not share it with your students?

Students often struggle with class work and need help acquiring the perseverance to stay on task and complete the work at hand. One day, in an effort to help my students with their struggles, I relayed the story of the woodpecker. "How many times does the woodpecker peck at a tree for food?" I asked. Their answers varied: 10? 100? 1000? 1,000,000?

Finally one well-intentioned student took the time to think through the question at hand. As his light bulb came on, he smiled and called out the answer I had been looking for: "Until he gets the job done!"

A woodpecker's work ethic isn't just important, it is vital to his survival. If he stops pecking before he gets the bugs from under the tree bark, he becomes weak from a lack of food. If his poor work ethic continues and the woodpecker gives up before his job is done, he will eventually die.

Staying with the woodpecker analogy, I explained to the students that their grades and their success in school depend on their own work ethic. This sparked an interesting and enlightening discussion. Soon, students were beginning to get the idea that a person's work ethic had long-reaching consequences for life.

This led to a creative exercise that helped reinforce the idea that perseverance pays off. Students took out their crayons and markers and began drawing pictures of big redheaded woodpeckers with the caption, "Keep pecking away!" By the end of class each student had a poster to take home and one to keep on display in the classroom.

It helped a lot! Jeffrey, a fourth grade student in my Character Class, came to school one day to tell me that he was mad at the woodpecker.

"He just won't leave me alone," he said. "Last night I came in from playing outside and had an hour until bedtime. I took a bath and got all ready to watch my favorite television show. Just as it came on, I realized that I hadn't done my homework. Now, I really wanted to watch that show! After thinking about it, I made up my mind to watch the show and let my homework go. Maybe I could get up early to do it in the morning before I left for school."

"How did you feel about that decision, Jeff?" I asked.

"I just couldn't do it, Ms. Brown," he said. "I was watching my favorite show, and there was that poster of the woodpecker on my bedroom door. I could just hear him peck-peck-pecking away. I finally turned off the television and finished my homework. I knew that I couldn't stop working on my homework until the job was done."

What a great ending!

> Real-life messages
> give the school a common language
> for building character.

Character messages are all around us and visual reminders can really help young children focus on those messages. In fact, visuals help teachers, too! Tuning in to the needs and interests of one's students is the first step to finding the metaphors and messages that will have a lasting impact. Creating the awareness of the natural messages in the environment is the second step. The application to the real lives of children follows.

After my success with the woodpecker, I went on the prowl for other meaningful metaphors that could reinforce the character messages I wanted my students to learn. I found several. Sharing these with you may help you with your own search.

Real-Life Character Messages

Light Bulb: Think about good character!

Exclamation Mark: Get excited about doing the right thing!

Woodpecker: Keep pecking away!

Picture Frame: Picture it! Picture yourself as a kid of character!

Magic Wand: There's no magic wand to acquiring good character. It takes work!

Building Blocks (A+B=C): Attitude + Behavior = Character

Mirror: Look for the best in others...and in yourself!

Star: Get the character habit! It will keep you in the company of stars!

Chalkboard and Eraser: Each day is a clean slate!

Toolbox: Stock your toolbox! (Stock it with good habits!)

Ruler and Yardstick: Measure up! (Measure up to your true potential!)

Doorknob: Run through open doors (of opportunity)!

Pencil: Write down your goals!

Basketball Net: Keep your eye on the goal!

Barbell: Pump yourself up with good character! (Strength training)

Target: Target practice helps!

Candle: Let your character shine through!

Broom: If we all sweep in front of our own doors, the whole school will be clean!

Sunglasses: Good character is so bright you'll need shades!

These real-life messages are wonderful tools for keeping your students on task. They serve as gentle reminders of powerful character lessons. When woven into the fabric of a school, they give students and teachers a common language for building character.

For example, students have stopped me in the cafeteria line just to say that they are *stocking their toolbox, pumping themselves up with good character*, or *getting excited about doing the right thing*. We're speaking the same language. And, it's a real joy to hear students speaking the language of good character with one another!

The first step is listening to the message. The next step is learning. Then comes the ultimate goal—living it. Living the example is always the best way to pass it on. Don't keep your light under a basket. Let it shine! Good character is so bright, you and your students *will* need shades!

Weaving the Fabric

Passing on the Message

As the school year progressed, my kindergarten students and I learned so much about the character message from our time together. I knew that the next step was passing it along to the other students in our school. My students also felt that we should not keep our character light hidden under a basket. We weren't sure how to get started, but we were looking for a way.

In a faculty meeting, the staff was planning whole-school monthly assemblies as a celebration for good behavior and academic responsibility. However, this first month there would be 24 students in our K–6 school who had not earned the privilege of attending. I volunteered to take the first detention duty. One of the teachers asked, "Deb, why don't you consider teaching some of your character lessons to the kids in detention? Instead of them just doing busy-work, you could begin working with them and give them the tools to work their way out of detention."

I thought that was a great idea! The staff agreed. And out of that idea, the Character Class was born at Lakewood Elementary!

Over the 1997-1998 school year, the class began growing. A change was in order. We didn't want the students to try to get into the class by breaking school rules. But the children who attended the Character Class were talking about it and other students began expressing an interest in visiting. They weren't sure what was going on in Room 111, but they wanted to check it out for themselves. The staff had to ask a serious question: Do we want the kids to *want* to attend detention in

> "The school not only has the opportunity to instill good character, it has the responsibility."
>
> —**Dr. B. David Brooks**

order to learn the character lessons? Perhaps it was time to change detention—and to open up the Character Class for students who wanted to attend.

Reflecting on the situation, I decided that a new game plan was in order and decided to give up my planning period on Thursdays. This opened up the Character Class to anyone who wanted to attend. Every other Thursday, I would go to the school intercom and announce, "The Character Class will meet today in Ms. Brown's classroom from 1:00 until 1:30. Everyone is invited!" Little did I know what would happen and how that simple announcement would change my life!

The class grew! At 1:00, the kids would start pouring in. Kindergartners, third graders, fifth graders. In they marched. They sat at tables, in extra chairs and on the floor. All were eager to learn. By winter, the class was bulging at the seams! There I was, alone in the classroom with 60 or more energetic students, yet I loved every minute!

Before long, another revision was in order. I expanded the class so we could meet every Thursday. At 1:00, students would begin streaming in! By spring more than 100 students were attending the class. By now, we were sitting everywhere, even on the windowsills! Had the fire marshal visited, there would have definitely been trouble! But I loved this class and didn't want to give it up. The children were respectful and well behaved and on task, learning the character message. What incredible excitement was in this room!

In an effort to reduce the large class numbers, the staff suggested that I divide the class into two groups—primary and intermediate. But I fought the suggestion. There was something very special about all of us being in there together. The principal and staff had noticed an increased rapport between older and younger students in the school. The younger children were looking up to the older kids for advice and example. And the older students were rising to the challenge! The younger children had learned that the older students really liked them and that they could learn from them, as well. The primary students felt they had an important contribution to make. Our school even saw better Buddy Projects going on than in previous years. We were really coming together as a school. The Character Class had helped build a new sense of unity throughout the school.

Out of desperation to keep the children together, I posted a note on the refrigerator door in the Teachers' Lounge. It read: "Teachers, Sign up here for a free planning period on Fridays. The Character Class is going on the road!" In addition to the Thursday class, I decided to give up my Friday planning period and take the class to other Lakewood classrooms. It took about 48 hours for the list on the refrigerator door to be filled with takers. Each Friday for the rest of the school year was booked.

At first, I thought that the teachers would leave the classroom for a well-deserved break while I was teaching their class. Little by little, I noticed that they were beginning to stay. They would sit at their desks and grade papers or work on lesson plans. But they were listening! It was a wonderful opportunity to model character teaching. It also helped them to become more confident in trying a few new things in their classrooms. It worked like magic and before I knew it, we had

> "The Character Class will meet today in Ms. Brown's classroom at one o'clock. Everyone is invited!"
>
> —Lakewood School intercom announcement

gathered a team of interested teachers who wanted to make the character message a part of the life of our school. So, out of the Character Class for students, the Lakewood Character Team of teachers was born. That was one of my happiest moments.

By the end of the school year, the Character Class had reached 253 of Lakewood's 357 students. Not a bad first year! Many teachers worried that I was sacrificing too much because I had "given up" my Thursday and Friday planning periods. Believe me, I didn't give up a thing! I was getting back much more than I gave. In addition to learning from the students, I was able to enjoy that wonderful feeling that comes from doing the right thing. And what I learned changed me forever.

Some assessment of the Character Class was now in order. We needed to revisit the original intent of the class, which was to help students become more responsible learners, so I did my homework. After collecting the data, the results were tallied and shared with the staff and parents. Here is what we discovered.

The Character Class

68.7% of students reported an improvement in behavior and responsibility.

65.6% of students reported academic improvement: more completed class work and homework assignments and had better weekly test scores and better report card grades.

Even parents said their children were showing better behavior at home and acting more responsibly. A favorite comment came from a parent who wondered how I had inspired her son to put his dirty clothes in the hamper, rather than leaving them in the usual places—on the floor and under his bed. It was heartwarming for me to see the character message was being learned and lived everywhere!

Moving On

During the spring of this wonderful year, I learned that I would lose my teaching position at Lakewood due to budget cuts and would not be able to teach there the following year. I was heartbroken. It was hard to hide my feelings from the students. Everyone was talking about it. Lakewood had never lost a teacher to staffing cuts in the thirty-five years the school had been open. Finally the day arrived when my Character Class kids asked me about it. They were very upset. I had to be honest with them.

"Who will teach the Character Class next year?" they asked. I had to say that I didn't know, but that I wanted it to continue. I had to prepare them, in case no staff member took it on. I asked them, "If no teacher steps up to the plate next year, how can we be sure that the character message will live on at Lakewood?"

One hundred and ten students looked at one another. I'll never forget the looks on their faces. Then, a fourth-grade student named Sarah gave us the hope we were looking for. "*We* will do it!" she said with conviction. It was what my weary heart was waiting to hear.

"Yes, you can help each other continue learning and living the message!" I told them. "*You* can make sure that the character message never dies."

One fifth-grade student continued, "Ms. Brown, will you promise us one thing?" I was almost afraid to answer. I really wasn't in a position to promise these kids anything for the next year.

"What is it, Andrew?" I asked.

"Will you promise us that wherever you are next year that you will teach the Character Class? If *we* can't have it, at least some other kids will get to."

That warmed my heart. You can guess what happened next...another *good* cry!

"Will you promise us that wherever you go next year—that you will teach the Character Class? If we can't have it, at least some other kids will get to."

—Andrew, age 10

The Smallest Gift

The last weeks of school brought many students and parents through my classroom door. They came with heavy hearts, bearing homemade cards and simple gifts. They brought feelings of disbelief, regret, and sadness. They came for goodbye hugs and to offer good wishes.

The last Tuesday of the school year, there was a knock on classroom door at the end of the day. It was a former student, Will, and his mother, Linda. Will had been in my kindergarten class the year before and had visited me faithfully after he started first grade. He always brought a smile and a first-grade hug when he came to visit. Will's mother said that he enjoyed stopping by to fill me in on all of his first-grade news. What Will didn't know was that his visits did more for me than they did for him!

This particular day Will stopped by with *the question.* "Ms. Brown, are you really leaving Lakewood?"

"Yes, I'm afraid so, Will. I don't want to, but I don't have a choice," I said sadly.

"Were you fired?" he wanted to know.

"No, Will, I wasn't fired, but I did lose my job because of cutbacks here at school," I tried to explain.

"Just tell them that you won't leave," suggested Will.

"I can't do that," I explained. "Even when it's hard, I have to show good character. I have to do the right thing."

"Well, I brought you a going-away gift," Will announced. "There are two pennies in this box," he explained, "and the dates on the pennies are very important. 1991 is the year I was born, and 1997 is the year you had me in your class. It was the year my life was changed."

"What do you mean, Will?" I asked.

He smiled and said, "It was the year that I learned to be a *kid of character*!"

At that point, I had another good cry. Here was Will, only seven years old and his life had been changed by the character message!

His mother added, "Deb, no matter how far away you are, you and Will always will be connected because you have his heart. He loves you so much. Thank you for all that you taught Will, but the character lessons are the lessons that mean the most to his dad and me."

That was a precious and uplifting moment in the midst of a heartbreaking time and evidence of the great power and promise in educating for character.

The school year ended. With a heavy heart, I packed up twenty-two years of teaching and moved it all home. With the last load in the trunk of my car, I drove out of the parking lot choked with emotion. As I looked into my rearview mirror, I took a last glance at the school marquee. It said simply, "Have a safe and fun summer. Character counts!" I felt a deep sense of pride that I'd left a legacy at Lakewood. Character *does* count in the school community. But it also counts in *every* community!

I'm happy to say that four weeks into the summer, I found a new job in a different hometown school, this time teaching sixth grade. As soon as that new school year started, I realized it was no coincidence that I had lost my job and was forced to move on. These children needed the character message, too, and I was proud to be the messenger!

Chapter Six

Growing in Goodness

A New Day

It was the first day of class at my new school. After eighteen years of teaching kindergarten, I was now facing the new challenge of working with sixth-grade students. It had been almost twenty years since I had taught an intermediate class. But I was ready for the challenge. Or at least thought that I was.

By seven o'clock in the morning, I could hear students pouring into the school building. Most were heading to the cafeteria for breakfast. I still had thirty minutes before they would enter my classroom and thought I had still had some time to think and mentally prepare for the day.

Then my classroom door opened. A young woman walked in wearing low-cut, black Spandex tights and stiletto heels. After my lengthy tour of duty teaching kindergarten, I wasn't even sure that I could spell *stiletto*. The woman had on a midriff top that was very low-cut, revealing lots of cleavage and tummy. Her dyed black-and-red hair was crafted with gel into a hair-raising punk style and her face was covered with thick layers of extreme make-up.

I got up from my desk, walked toward her, extended my hand and introduced myself. "Good morning!' I said. "My name is Deb Brown. I'm the new sixth grade teacher here at Weimer. Do you have a student in my class?"

Appearing quite puzzled, she looked at me and rolled her eyes. "I *am* the student in your class!"

"Education has for its object the formation of character."

—**Herbert Spencer**

Taking a deep breath, I realized there was no time now for mental preparation and tried to quickly adjust to the fact that school had started.

"What is your name?" I asked.

"My name is April," she answered.

I put my hand on her shoulder and said softly. "April, I am glad that you will be in my class. But you cannot come to my classroom dressed this way."

"Why?" was her quick retort.

"For two reasons," I explained. "First of all, out of respect for yourself. I want for you to be a successful learner. And self-respect is the foundation for all learning. Second, out of respect for this school, its rules, and all that it stands for. Now if you will go into the restroom and take off some of that make-up, I will go to the counselor's closet and find you a shirt to wear today to cover up with. As for the shoes, I'm afraid you are on your own. And I think that, after physical education class a little later in the day, tomorrow you might wish to consider a more comfortable alternative." With that, I smiled and touched her arm reassuringly.

Throughout that first day, April was distant and cool. She didn't say much, but watched my every move. Whenever our eyes met, I would always smile back. And whenever I passed by her seat, I would lightly pat her on the shoulder.

I tried to make this first day of school comfortable and enjoyable for everyone. For a few minutes in the afternoon, I took the class outside for recess and some social interaction. April was on the basketball court shooting hoops in those high-heeled shoes. I couldn't resist the opportunity to break the ice and went over to her and said gently, "At a time like this, I bet you are missing your tennis shoes!"

She smiled at me and almost laughed.

At the end of the day, I peeked inside April's journal: "The first day of school got off to a bad start.... I didn't think I would like my new teacher...but I think she might really care about us. I think it will be OK."

I took a deep breath and sighed with relief.

A New Challenge

Soon after school started, one of my new sixth-grade students asked a question that changed my entire outlook on everything. It was right after lunch and the question took away my innocence as a teacher and made me realize that my previous twelve years of teaching kindergarten had shielded me from the real world of older students.

"When are we going to talk about Jerry Springer?" a female student wanted to know.

I wasn't sure that I was hearing correctly. "Talk about *what*?" I asked.

"About *The Jerry Springer Show*!" was the enthusiastic response.

"Who in this class watches Jerry Springer?" I asked. Each and every hand went up. "How often do you watch?" I had to ask.

"Every day!" they said.

I remember getting cold chills and realized, as the room fell silent, that this was a defining moment for me with my students. I proceeded carefully.

One student volunteered to tell the story of fifth grade. Each evening after school, the students would go home and turn on the TV. For an hour, they would watch this particular show. Not some of them, but all of them. The next day at school they would discuss the show and talk about what they had seen. Of course, these were lighthearted and fun-poking discussions about the program, its guests, the fighting, and the bad language. The students had come to expect these discussions in school and looked forward to them as an opportunity to talk about their personal lives.

I asked them why they were such avid fans.

"Because it's funny!" came the unanimous answer.

"*The Jerry Springer Show* is awesome! *Everybody* watches it!" one student said.

"Tell me about it," I said. And tell me, they did.

Then I listened with a heavy heart to their stories of aired family fights, secret affairs, same-sex couples who had cheated with the opposite sex, young adults who claimed affairs with multiple partners, and young girls who didn't even know the heritage of their children.

At the end of the telling, silence returned to our classroom. The students were looking to me for a comment. I had to remember that this was just the first week of school and knew that my response would set the tone for the rest of the school year. Looking upward for strength, tears started down my cheeks. Searching for the right words for these eleven- and twelve-year-old children, I said simply, "Now I know."

Every face was fixed on me. I continued, "Now I know why I lost my job at Lakewood and ended up here. You need to hear the message." Then I walked to the front of the room, picked up a piece of chalk, and wrote two words on the chalkboard: "Last year." Then I turned and asked the students to read it aloud.

"Last year," the class responded in unison. Without saying a word, I simply picked up the eraser and erased their past.

Not a word was spoken. But I could tell from the looks on their faces that they didn't know what to think. Then I explained.

"Last year is gone," I said. "This is a new year. This is the year we will learn the character message. Any questions?"

One brave soul raised her hand. "Ms. Brown, do *you* watch Jerry Springer?"

"What would be your guess?" I asked the class.

"Probably not..." was the consensus.

Gently, but with conviction, I told them, "No, I do not watch it."

Another student asked, "Why not?"

I gave these inquiring students a thoughtful response. "Let me share with you a little something that a very wise friend, Dr. Mitchell, once taught me," I said. "After you watch any television show, turn off the set for just a moment and ask yourself this question: I have just traded an hour of my life for this show. Can I say that it was a good trade?" Then I added my own personal question: *"Does this show*

> "After you watch any television show, turn off the set for just a moment and ask yourself this question: I have just traded an hour of my life for this show. Can I say that it was a good trade?"
>
> —Dr. William Mitchell

help me with my goal to become a better student and a better person? If it doesn't, I turn it off—for good. If it does, then I try to be sure to watch it the next time that it comes on."

I challenged my students, "Just promise me that whenever you watch television that you will think about it and ask yourself those same, important questions. Just become reflective about the shows you watch. Then you can make good decisions—decisions that will help your life to become better, decisions that will help you reach your new goals of personal and academic excellence." With that said, I went right on to the next item on the day's agenda: "Get out your social studies books..."

The sixth graders and I were on our way to learning academics a new way. I had the secret to success tucked away in my heart. Teaching for character translates academically. It was now time to share that with a new class and a new school. I smiled as I took on the challenge. It felt good to finally know that losing my job at Lakewood was part of a bigger plan. It helped melt away some of the pain. I now felt the needed sense of belonging to this new school and this new class. And it was a great feeling.

Reflecting back to something I had read in Tom Lickona's wonderfully wise book, *Educating for Character*, I recalled this quote: "Schools teach character every day by design or default." I had the feeling that my carrying the character message to this particular class was part of the grand design.

Building a Foundation

It was time to start building a foundation for learning with my new sixth-grade students. I knew that they needed some good role models to help them with their journey to personal and academic excellence and thought back to when I was their age. I remembered thinking that heroes were dead presidents and statesmen who had made a difference in our country's history. I knew that these students needed more than that. They needed to learn about real people who are alive now, making a real difference in the world. And one of the messages that I wanted them to learn is that they had heroic qualities within themselves and that they could be heroes, too. So I started with the story of Frank Daily.

Frank Daily was a fourteen-year-old student who lived in the city of Milwaukee. He was an athlete, who wanted to make the basketball team more than anything. Frank and his mother had saved their pennies until the grand day when Frank could buy the basketball shoes of his dreams!

One cold, gray December day, Frank and his friends were riding the Milwaukee city bus home after basketball practice. The temperatures were well below freezing, and it had been snowing for most of the day.

The bus jerked to a stop in front of the County Institutions grounds. A very pregnant woman slowly pulled herself onto the bus by the

handrail. As she fell backward into her seat, her feet kicked up—and Frank could see that she was in her stocking feet.

As the bus driver steered the bus back into traffic, he yelled back over his shoulder, "Hey, lady! Where are your shoes? It ain't more than ten degrees out there!"

"I can't afford shoes," the woman answered. She pulled her fraying coat collar around her neck. Some of the boys on the bus exchanged glances and smirked. "I just got on the bus to get my feet warm," the woman continued. "If you don't mind, I'll just ride around with you for a bit."

The bus driver scratched his bald head. "How come you can't afford shoes?"

"I got eight kids," she said. "They all got shoes. There's not enough left for me."

Frank looked down at his new Nike basketball shoes. His feet were warm and snug. And then he looked back at the woman. Her socks were ripped. Her coat, missing buttons, hung open around her belly—covered by a dirty dress. Frank felt a warm thawing in his gut. He probably would always be able to afford shoes. The woman probably never would. Under his seat, he pried the toe of one shoe into the heel of the other and slipped it off. Then the other shoe. He looked around. No one had noticed. He would have to walk three blocks home in the snow. But the cold had never bothered him much.

When the bus stopped at the end of the line, Frank waited until everyone else had emptied off. Then he reached under his seat and picked up his basketball shoes. He walked up to the woman at the front of the bus, looked down at her, gave her the shoes and said, "Here, lady...you need these more than I do."

And then Frank hurried to the door and stepped down. He managed to land in a puddle. It didn't matter. He wasn't at all cold. As he started to walk away he heard the woman exclaim, "See, they fit me just perfect!"

It was then that he heard the bus driver call out, "Hey, kid, come back here! What's your name?"

Frank said quietly, "My name is Frank Daily." "Well, Frank," said the bus driver, "I've been driving this bus for more than twenty years, and I've never seen anything like that in all those years."

The woman was crying. "Thank you, young man," she said.

Frank mumbled, "You're welcome." He smiled at the woman. "It's no big deal. Besides, it's almost Christmas."

Frank hurried off to catch up with his friends. It seemed to him that the grayness of the skies had lifted. On the way home, he hardly felt the cold beneath his feet at all.

—Excerpt from *Kids With Courage*, by Barbara Lewis
Free Spirit Publishing, copyright 1997

Frank Daily was a wonderful place to start! He was a real-life hero. What was more important to these sixth graders, he was someone with whom they could identify. I am proud to report that three months after hearing that story, one of my sixth-grade students measured up to the example set by Frank Daily.

Matt was celebrating his twelfth birthday at McDonald's with his family and had been given $25 and some nice gifts as birthday presents. While Matt and his family were eating dinner, he noticed a woman sitting alone in a corner of the restaurant. She looked poor, tired, and hungry. Like Frank Daily, Matt got that gnawing feeling in his gut. He was moved to action. He got up, walked over to that woman and gave her his $25 gift. Now, I wasn't there the day that Matt showed his character and compassion. But I can only guess that the look of gratitude on the face of that woman was Matt's best birthday gift of all!

Growing Together

There were many challenges throughout that first year at Weimer Elementary School. These students were taking several steps forward and then a huge step back. And it was easy to understand. The research is clear. A child's value system is in place by the age of ten. And here I was, bringing a new message to students at the age of eleven and twelve. I often wondered if I had arrived too late in their lives to make a difference.

But, I am a positive thinker and believe in hope, as well as the power of planting seeds. I also believe that even when the character message isn't taught at home, a teacher can still make a difference in a child's life. If I didn't believe that, I would be on the first bus leaving the teaching profession.

It's just that if you are late in your delivery, it is harder for children to learn the message. But it *can* happen! You just have to work harder. You have to be clear. You have to be consistent. And, more than anything else, you have to be patient and persevere and hang on to your own moral rope. You have to continue on, doing the right thing. Then, little by little, good things will begin to happen.

Growing in knowledge and character is a journey. It doesn't happen overnight. It takes time. It takes work. It takes wisdom. And it takes lots of love along the way. I helped my Weimer students with their journey, just like I helped my Lakewood kids. I loved them through the tough times! And it worked.

No, not every student earned a spot on the Honor Roll. Not every student made good decisions all of the time. Not every student gave away his birthday money to a person in need. But every kid did make small, but important, steps in his own journey toward goodness. It was my job to notice, appreciate, and cherish each of those incremental successes. It was also my job to cheer them on!

Celebrating Character!

During my first two years at Weimer, the character message spread. It left the sixth-grade classroom and traveled down school hallways. It permeated each and every part of our school as both teachers and students came on board. Our monthly Character Assemblies and Character Classes ensured that we were *all* growing in the character wisdom. A wonderful enthusiasm spread throughout the entire school community! It was a proud and humble moment when our school was given the district's first annual School of Character Award. More than the monetary part of the award, more than the recognition, the banner meant the most to me.

These four years later, that award banner hangs proudly on the outside of our school building, boldly proclaiming the character message. I hope that every person who passes by notices it and thinks about the meaning of the message. That banner, coupled with the school marquee, helps to send a clear message to our community about what is really important in our school.

Inside the school walls, we are calling our students to personal and academic excellence with the character message. There is power, magic, excitement, and promise in teaching for character. Please don't miss out on the adventure!

The Impact of Teaching For Character: A Kid Story

Meet Erin, a third-grade student in a suburban elementary school. From the time Erin was in kindergarten, she was shy and withdrawn. She never came to school prepared. Her empty backpack hung on its hook in the locker. There was never a completed homework assignment tucked inside. Neither was there a lunch, or even a mid-morning snack.

Erin lives with her young, unmarried mother and her grandfather in a rural trailer on a muddy road. Her mom is overwhelmed by life and often leaves the raising of young Erin and her brother to their rigid grandfather. He is negative and critical—on a good day.

These days in the third grade are the same as those in previous years. Only now, Erin is more withdrawn than ever. As the school year begins, so does the cycle of irresponsibility, poor behavior, and failing grades. After only six weeks of school, Erin is in academic trouble. Attempts to conference with her mother are unanswered. At the first school-wide celebration for good behavior and responsibility, Erin finds herself in detention for the hour with other familiar students who have also failed to measure up.

The teachers at this school are implementing character education for the first time this year. A faculty decision is made to use the detention time to teach and reinforce character lessons with the students. Beginning in October, the class meets twice a month. The teacher, using good character traits as the focus, begins working on the importance of a positive attitude in building for the future. As good habits are learned and reinforced, goals are thought out and written down. Little by little, Erin begins to see a possibility of breaking her tradition of irresponsibility, poor choices, and academic failure.

In the character class, the teacher looks for the best in the students and believes in them until they can come to believe in themselves. The character message is clear, the sentiment sincere. One day, Erin's third-grade teacher sends her to show her homework to the teacher of the character class. The assignment is complete, accurate, and neatly done. Erin smiles as the well-earned praise and recognition are bestowed! Now, she has a foundation for building.

Over the next months, the progress is slow, but steady. Erin is gaining in confidence and character. Frequent visits to the teacher of the character class and to the principal help support her in her efforts. The character class continues meeting and Erin now looks forward to those meetings. While waiting in the cafeteria line, Erin feels the character teacher's hand on her shoulder and knows that she has unconditional understanding, caring, and support in the classroom and beyond. She does not have to carry her academic and behavioral burdens alone.

In February during her planning period, the third-grade teacher is filing student work. She notices that Erin has not missed a single homework assignment in the last month. All of her assignments have been turned in. The work has been complete, neat, and a joy to grade. There are even a few perfect scores on weekly spelling tests. Erin's grades have slowly but steadily climbed from the *D* and *E* range to a good solid *B*. And Erin's behavior chart has been violation-free for the last several weeks!

Erin is now smiling more. She tells the teacher that she likes this new feeling that she has inside. She holds her head up as she walks down the hallways of school and down the muddy roads of life. She participates in class now, and she continues to grow in knowledge, character, self-respect, and goodness. Character education has made a difference in this young girl's life. Once Erin came to value and believe in herself, anything became possible—even academic success! As Erin came to understand the character message of respect, responsibility, caring, and hard work, a bigger and better thing happened. She came to *believe* it and then *live* it! And that has made all of the difference.

2
PART

The
Strategies

Character
in the Classroom

*"Education works, character can be taught and learned,
and teachers are our greatest hope of instilling good character
in this and the next generation."*
—**Dr. B. David Brooks**

After reading about my journey with kids, you may be interested in trying some ideas for yourself. These last two chapters are a compilation of tried-and-true philosophies and practices fresh from the classroom trenches. Included are some of my favorites and some of the students' favorites. When I work with other schools, my students always remind me to include their favorite character lessons and activities. "Don't forget to tell them about our last Character Assembly...the new bulletin board that we made...the new Character Card that we thought up," they will say. From their enthusiastic comments, it is evident that we've all enjoyed learning these character lessons. It's also evident that the kids now see themselves as character messengers, too!

The ideas on these pages really do work. Just thinking about them and writing them down helped me recall many happy experiences in the classroom with my students. Seeing them learn and grow in knowledge and goodness has brought me great joy! It has inspired me to always try to take the high road in my own life. Tom Lickona, a leading expert in character education, was right when he said that you can't teach good character unless you live it! I keep his words taped to my desk as a reminder of that awesome challenge.

The purpose of sharing these ideas is to get you excited about the possibilities and move you to action in your classroom. This will also help you see the wonderful things that you are already doing and move you to more intentional ways of teaching for character. After you finish reading this book, the next step is to roll up your sleeves. Start smiling and get to work with the kids in your life!

Chapter Seven

Building Climate

1 This Room Is Different!

"Little by little does the trick."

—Aesop

Seeing is believing. When students walk into your classroom for the very first time, their initial impression is very important. What they see matters. You can convey your heartfelt philosophy on learning and life by the way you decorate your classroom. This is a great climate-builder. When I changed schools a few years ago, the message was delivered to me in powerful ways. I moved into my new classroom and set it up during the month of July when school was out. Then, when everyone returned to school in August, it was interesting to watch the reactions when people saw my classroom for the very first time. Teachers, for example, walking by to say hello, would glance in, leave, then back up and look in again. The reaction was always the same. "What a great classroom!" they would say. Then they would come in for a closer look. This classroom was different, in part because there was so much to see! They often commented that they liked the blending of personal, professional, and academic themes in my room.

How your classroom is decorated and organized speaks volumes about you as a teacher and a person. You spend a lot of time in that room, so decorate it so that you and your students will feel right at home!

Color is important. Use color to make your classroom cheerful and bright. And let the light shine in! Pull the curtains or blinds back to let the light invite students into their new surroundings. Color and light are effective mood and attitude elevators that will help everyone feel better during their time in your room.

Organization is important, too. Having a place for everything emphasizes the importance of responsibility and models organizational skills in learning. Being organized will also support the development of classroom procedures with your students. If everything has its place, students will know what to do to become responsible!

2 The Personal Touch

Tables promote social-skill development and cooperative-learning skills. They are also great for discussions, large projects, and student artwork. For these and other reasons, I strongly recommend tables over individual student desks. Their versatility is an important part of the way I teach. There are large tables that seat six students and smaller tables that seat four, or even two. I also set up tables where students can sit to work alone.

Around my room are large area rugs and floor pillows. Nearby are baskets of clipboards. These are set up as specific areas where students can go for reading, research, and study. Small groups of students can also go there to discuss and record information. An individual student can go there to think and to work independently. These areas give students a break from sitting in a hard chair all day. They can stretch out and be comfortable and go on with the learning at hand.

Personal touches fill my classroom. In the center of my round computer table is a large green-and-white beach umbrella, open to invite students to the four classroom computers for daily curriculum reinforcement and research. It helps me to feel that my own personal beach is not so far away. On the opposite classroom wall is my beach window. For years I had asked our school secretary, Joanne, to requisition a window for my classroom. "And throw in a truckload of sand, a few palm trees and some salt water," was my usual request. For obvious reasons, the school district never built a beach outside my West Virginia classroom. So my kindergarten aide and I decided to take matters into our own hands! Pat, my teacher's aide, took molding and made a large picture frame that looked like a window. I painted a beach scene on large art paper and we attached it to the inside of the frame. Pat sewed a colorful valance and we hung it on a curtain rod over our newly constructed beach window, which we hung on the classroom wall. Now, a trip to the beach is never more than a glance away!

In different nooks and crannies around the classroom I place lighthouses, sailboats and seashells. These personal touches decorate the room and tell about me as a person. I have found that by sharing a little of myself with the students, they are comfortable sharing more of themselves with me. I keep a personal bulletin board near my desk filled with quotes, love notes, souvenirs and pictures of my home, family, friends, and special times in my life. The students love it! During break and snack time, they often stand and look at it while they eat and talk to their friends. They often ask me about the things on that board. The conversations that have started because of that bulletin board have been important in developing a comfortable and trusting relationship with my students. Near the end of the school year, students usually bring cameras to take pictures of their classroom and friends.

Without fail, pictures are always taken of this bulletin board. The first time this happened, I was puzzled. A student named Sarah had just taken a photograph of the board. When I asked her why, she said, "I just always want to remember this."

A life-sized poster of basketball great Larry Bird has hung in my classroom for years. Larry's days with the Boston Celtics are a proud example of the work ethic that I want all of my students to develop. Years later, students will come back to my classroom to see if Larry Bird and the beach umbrella are still there. Kids remember! They may not remember all that you taught them, but they will remember what kind of teacher you were and the classroom environment. Put some of yourself into your classroom. It will be a rich and rewarding experience!

Perhaps the most important section of my classroom is the area on the front of my desk where I post a collection of personal handmade messages, designed to reassure the students that I care. The messages say:

These subtle messages convey your commitment, love and caring for students. They get the message! We all are bombarded with visual messages in our day-to-day lives. In society, our print-rich environment is filled with advertising slogans and campaigns. Magazines, newspapers, television, and billboards all prove that visual messages work. Why not do a little advertising of your own? Fill your room with wisdom! Plaster your room with character messages. Put them everywhere. Make sure that they are neat, bright, colorful, and attractive. The kids will do the rest. The messages that you display will go far in helping your students internalize the character message. Reading the room is powerful indeed. Please don't miss out on the adventure!

3 A Golden Rule Classroom

The wall says it all: *This is a Golden Rule Classroom!* It is one of the first signs that you see when you enter my classroom and the foundation for all that I teach and for all that I do. Let your students know that you stand for the Golden Rule!

When I first started teaching in 1972, almost all of my students knew the meaning of the Golden Rule. It was taught at home and reinforced in schools, churches, civic organizations, and communities. These years later, things are very different. Many children have never heard of the Golden Rule, which in various phrasings is: "Treat others the way you would like to be treated." In fact, most *don't* know what it is. Four years ago when, I started teaching at Weimer Elementary, I asked my students about the Golden Rule on the first day of school. Sadly, only one student out of twenty-five had heard of the Golden Rule. However, it wasn't long before every student in that class came to know and understand this important rule. And I am thrilled to report that, four years later, every student in our school now knows what it is. It's a great rule for all of us to follow.

4 Good Morning!

When students enter the classroom each morning, I am there at the door to greet them with a warm welcome. "Good morning! I'm glad you're here!" is a wonderful way to start the day. Students feel noticed, valued, and affirmed by the greeting. Hal Urban calls this practice *transferring positive energy at the door*, and Charlie Abourjilie calls it his daily *handshake*. Both of these master teachers, character authors, and national speakers know the power of that personal greeting. A hug, handshake, high-five, or touch on the shoulder let students know that you care. Calling students by name is the icing on the cake. Dale Carnegie taught that the sweetest sound to anyone is the sound of his own name. John Dewey and William James taught that the deepest need in human nature is to be valued, appreciated, and affirmed. The morning greeting takes these important teachings and puts them into practice for the students in your life. If something happens to prevent you from being there when students enter your classroom, make a point to make eye contact with them and convey a personal remark at some point before class is over. At the end of the day, make sure you have had a personal moment of interaction with each and every student. Remember, in our busy and task-filled lives, the most important element in teaching is still the *human* element!

5 The Sound of Music

Music creates a wonderful climate for learning. Classical music stimulates the brain, fosters creativity, and makes some learning tasks easier and more fun. I always have music playing when students enter my classroom. It helps set the stage for whatever I have planned. Sometimes it's upbeat, sometimes it's a soft and soothing instrumental. I play music when students enter, when they leave, and sometimes in-between. Students will often ask for classical music when they are doing dictionary research, math problems, or artwork. I gladly oblige because it helps them relax, get motivated, and stay on task. At the end of the day, especially on Fridays, we get into my favorites—the oldies! This helps all of us leave for the day on a positive and upbeat note!

6 On Your Feet!

I seldom use my desk. I think it is my job to be with my students, teaching, modeling, moving around, offering help, answering questions, and cheering them on. There are times when I sit at my desk—for example, early in the morning before students arrive, when taking the lunch count and attendance, during my planning period, and at the end of the school day. After school, I'll sit down to reflect on the day's learning and review what went well, as well as what didn't, as I prepare for the next day. But the rest of the school day is spent on my feet. It's a long day and I do get tired, so I wear comfortable shoes. I also lean from time to time on the countertop near my classroom sink. Or I'll half-sit for a bit on the edge of a table. But my feet are planted firmly on the floor. The point is, I don't teach from behind a desk. An *up and at 'em* approach to teaching says a lot to students about attitude, caring, and work ethic.

7 Called to Rise

Set the stage for all you do by establishing student expectations. It is a teacher's *job* to teach academics, but it is also a teacher's *duty* to teach character. My goal for my students and myself is personal and academic excellence. Each year, we embark on a journey to become better students and better people. Most teaching professionals believe that it is our responsibility to *call* our students to excellence. But how do we do that?

> - Believe in your students and look for the best.
> - Do more than lead...inspire.
> - Motivate them.
> - Model for them and show them the way.
> - Teach them.
> - Guide them.
> - Encourage them.
> - Accept only their best effort.
> - Listen to them.
> - Enable them to succeed.
> - Pick them up whenever they fall.

I remember a time that I asked a new class of students this question: "Anyone can be average. Is that all that you want to be?" Now this was a class of underachievers, and their response really surprised me, "Yeah! We usually make D's and E's. If we could make C's, that would be great! Our parents would get off of our backs!"

I talked with the students about the difference between mediocrity and excellence, and I explained that we would be taking the higher road. In the classroom over the doorway, I posted a poem by Emily Dickinson, "Called To Rise." That poem has made all the difference. Daily, it calls each student to rise to personal as well as academic excellence.

Called To Rise
by Emily Dickinson

We never know how high we are
'Til we are called to rise.
And then if we are true to plan
Our statures touch the skies.

8 Give Out Your Telephone Number

Yes, you read that correctly! The first day of school, I walk around to each student and write my name and telephone number on the inside cover of his or her student assignment notebook. In my own handwriting, in blue ink, it says:

Deb A. Brown
727-7888

This is one of the most rewarding practices I use with my students. First, it lets students know that I care about them beyond the school walls and beyond the school day. Then I give them direction and guidance for using this number. I tell them it is for a time when they might really need me. It is not for social calls or interruptions to my family life. But it can also be used if their parents need me. I ask that they not call after 9:00 p.m., as a simple matter of respect. A fellow teacher once criticized the practice by saying that I should write my name as Ms. Brown, rather than Deb. But the use of my first name is very deliberate. This is the way my name is listed in the telephone directory. After seeing it written this way in their assignment book each day for an entire school year, students remember how my number is listed and can look me up long after they leave my classroom.

Has this practice ever been abused? Only a few times. One night a parent called near midnight on a school night and woke me up to ask about a permission slip for a class field trip, and a couple of times students called to play a prank. But as you get further along with your character teaching, students and parents both begin to develop a respect for you that weeds out late-night and unimportant phone calls. After twenty-six years of teaching, I can count on one hand the phone calls that were untimely or disrespectful. That's not a bad record.

Have their been rewards for this practice? Absolutely! One Friday night, a sixth-grade student called to say that she had been left alone at home while her parents were out of town. Her older brother had been told to watch her but was nowhere to be found and Crystal was afraid. I spent some time talking with her. At the end of that conversation, who do you think felt better—my student or me? Another time, a twelve-year-old student who had been written up for being disrespectful earlier in the day called to ask if I had a minute to listen. Zack pointed out that he was referring to the sign on my desk that says *I love you enough to listen*. I assured him that I did have time. Although he had made a mistake at school, Zack wanted me to know that he was a good kid. "I want you to see another side of me," Zack said. He got his violin and played one of his favorite songs, *Jesus Loves Me*. As I sat and listened to that beautiful music, the tears streamed down my face. I wouldn't have missed that for the world!

And there was Ashley, a tenderhearted student who had a change of conscience after the dismissal bell. She called me at home to admit that she hadn't been completely honest on a math assignment the students had graded for themselves. After thinking about it, she decided to come clean. I know that Ashley felt better after calling me at home to clear the slate.

9 Classroom Procedures: They're Just Routine!

Classroom procedures are crucial to the smooth running of a class and give structure to the day. The result is that there is more time to teach and more time to learn. The first week of school is the time to teach your classroom procedures. This involves teaching, modeling, and re-teaching. Then we practice and practice and practice! *Practice makes perfect!* We practice how to enter and exit the room quietly and respectfully, how to line up, and how to travel the hallways. We practice our arrival routine, our lunch-time routine, our dismissal routine, going to our lockers, entering the classroom, graphing in for lunch and attendance, putting our homework and notes from home in the proper basket, and taking out our Character Journals to begin our day. We spend the first week of school practicing these basic procedures so that we can have the other 175 days of school for instruction! The result? Good habits are built around this classroom structure. Students know what to do and when. If you see your students starting to slip later in the school year, take time to practice. Reminders are sometimes needed after Christmas or spring vacation. Eventually, the routines become second nature to your students. They become confident and secure. And then, you can get on with the learning!

10 The Teacher Pledge

The very first week of school, I initiate a class discussion on what makes a good teacher. I take a large sheet of chart paper and some large colored markers and record the students' ideas. The more we talk, the more I write. I want to record their every thought. Each year, the students come up with wonderful ideas and the process makes it easy to see what character traits are important to them. I take that chart home and use it to make a pledge. I write down the teacher traits that I promise to use in the classroom in an effort to achieve my goal as a good teacher. I group them according to the character traits that each idea represents. Then, I sign the pledge. The new chart is laminated and posted in the classroom—and referred to often during the school year. I use it as a measuring stick for how well I am doing and as motivation to achieve personal and professional excellence. The students feel comfortable and safe because of my promise.

Teacher Pledge		
	Respect	I will listen to my students.
		I will speak in a soft and respectful voice.
	Responsibility	I will grade and return papers in a timely manner.
		I will give only important, valuable assignments.
	Caring	I will help each student who asks for help.
		I will plan interesting and fun learning activities/lessons.
	Fairness	I will treat each student fairly, without prejudice.
		I will be available to answer student questions.
	Trustworthiness	I will honor student confidentiality.
	Citizenship	I will be a good role model for kids.
		I will make contributions for the good of our school.

11 The Student Pledge

This follow-up activity will initiate a discussion about what makes a good class. Using the traits of good character as a guide, the students and I talk about their responsibilities and behavior and the resulting effect on classroom learning. Again, I encourage them to share their ideas and then record what they have to say on a large chart paper. From that brainstorming session, we make a pledge with one another. Much discussion occurs about the character trait that each idea represents and we learn a lot about the meaning of each trait as we move through the discussion. After the pledge is copied on a neat and colorful poster, each student signs the pledge. This chart is also posted in the room, so that students have a reminder and motivation for living up to their promise. Because the ideas were theirs, students have ownership in the pledge. It becomes a meaningful part of their quest for personal and academic excellence.

Student Pledge		
	Respect	I will listen when the teacher is talking.
		I will listen when a classmate is talking.
		I will follow The Golden Rule.
		I will show good manners.
	Responsibility	I will complete and turn in assignments on time.
		I will come prepared for class.
		I will stay on task.
	Caring	I will be thoughtful of my classmates.
		I will share with my classmates.
		I will help my classmates.
	Fairness	I will take turns with my classmates.
		I will include all of my classmates and will not leave anyone out.
	Trustworthiness	I will not cheat.
		I will not lie.
		I will tell the whole truth.
		I will not take things that do not belong to me.
	Citizenship	I will not litter our school.
		I will recycle paper.
		I will do my patrol duty with honor.

12 Caught and Taught

There has been a great deal of discussion among educators about whether good character is caught or taught. I believe that both answers are correct. Good character is *taught* by the intentional teaching of the traits of good character. It is also *caught* by the examples that teachers model. It is not enough simply to teach and espouse the lessons of good character. We must also demonstrate good character. Students will remember what we say and what we do. As Dr. Tom Lickona so brilliantly wrote in his book, *Educating for Character*, schools teach character each day by design or default. So be intentional, rather than incidental, with your modeling and teaching.

13 Morning Announcements

Character in the morning is a wonderful thing! When the tardy bell rings, the morning announcements begin. Two students come on over the school intercom and the magic begins.

"Good morning! Today is Thursday, December 4th. We are Julie and Misty, and we are in the sixth grade. We will be doing our morning announcements. Please stand for the Pledge to the Flag. [All students in the school stand and say the patriotic pledge together. The school comes alive with excitement!] And now we will say the Weimer Pledge: I will act in such a way that I will be proud of myself and others will be proud of me, too. I came to school to learn, and I will learn. I will have a good day.

"We will now say The Cultivating Character Steps To Success. Please repeat them after me: Be confident. Be responsible. Be here. Be on time. Be friendly. Be polite. Be a listener. Be prepared. Be a doer. Be a tough worker. Be a risk taker. Be healthy. Be a goal setter.

"Our character quote for today is: 'There are two ways to get to the top of an oak tree. You can climb the branches, or you can sit on an acorn and wait.'

"Our morning announcements are: Today is the 47th day of school. Recycling is due at 8:00. We'd like to thank our librarian, Miss Clifton, for her wonderful work on our school book fair. Our Character Assembly will be held this afternoon at 1:00 in the cafeteria. Please return the parent surveys that are due on Friday. Happy birthday to Mr. Handley, our principal. We love you!

"We hope that you all have a good day growing in knowledge and growing in character. Remember to know the good, love the good and do the good!"

In this way our day begins. What a wonderful sound it is to hear the character message resounding through the school so early in the morning! It sets the stage for all we do in the classroom that day. With a start like that, the instructional day looks more promising than ever!

14 The Morning Meeting

It is important to start the day off together. The Morning Meeting is a way to do that. Right after the morning announcements, we all come together for the meeting. The students usually sit on the rug and lean back on the big, comfortable floor pillows. I sit in a chair close by. At that time, I make announcements and give students any information they need to take home to their parents. We also share and celebrate good news. Hitting a home run at last night's ball game or getting a new puppy is always more fun when shared with friends. Some days there is bad news to share. A family illness or death is sad to share, but is an important part of our caring curriculum. Some days we describe funny things that have happened and share about our lives outside of the classroom. This process is a real community builder. It may just be my favorite part of the day. Taking five minutes for this activity will set the stage for students to be on task for the day's learning. Trust me, it is time well spent!

15 Basic School Civilities

During the first weeks of school, when I am training my students with rules and procedures, I create an awareness of respect for others. A colleague of mine, Barbara Walters, once taught a graduate class on self-respect and resiliency. I took the class and found that many resiliency skills are closely related to character development. One thing Barbara said has stayed with me over the years: *How we treat one another matters.* How simple, yet profound. Those five little words have helped guide me in the way that I teach and the way that I live.

It is important to teach students the basic civilities that make school a nicer place to work and learn. We start off making a chart at the beginning of the school year and we add to it as we go along. By living and learning together, we came up with a list that serves us well.

> "How we treat one another matters."
>
> **—Barbara Walters**
> Student Assistance
> Program Coordinator
> Kanawha County Schools,
> West Virginia

1. Saying *please* and *thank you*
2. Saying *sir* and *ma'am* when speaking with adults
3. Smiling at people we see at school
4. Greeting people and saying *hello*
5. Opening doors for others
6. Giving others space in line
7. Answering adults when they speak to you
8. Being polite at every opportunity
9. Showing respect at all times

16 School Quiet Times

Building a climate that is conducive to learning requires that some parts of the school day be *quiet times*. For many years of teaching, I simply wove those requirements into my classroom rules. And for many of those years, students fought me on it. They would break the rules by talking in the halls, during fire drills, and in line. What bothered me the most was student talking when another teacher came into my room to ask me a question.

By weaving the character message into the fabric of your classroom, you will eventually find that fewer students are breaking the quiet-times rule. Why? Because by teaching character, you build a foundation of respect. Once my students understood that being quiet at certain times was a sign of respect, they were happier to comply. It was such a simple thing, yet it made so much difference!

As a class, we brainstormed about the times that we really *needed* to remain quiet. As usual, I recorded their responses. Together, we came up with a list of quiet times for our class and our school. This list was shared with the rest of the school through our monthly Character Class and Character Assemblies. With teacher cooperation and student buy-in, this list has helped our school maintain a more orderly learning environment.

School Quiet Times
Staying quiet at these times shows our respect.

1. During a fire drill
2. During a shelter-in-place drill
3. During school intercom announcements
4. When a visitor enters the classroom
5. When the teacher is talking or teaching
6. During silent reading time
7. During a test
8. In line
9. In the school hallways

---

17 Teacher Modeling

Teacher modeling is a most important part of the teaching and learning process, as the following true story illustrates. One day, during a kindergarten school year, my aide and I were taking our students to the cafeteria for lunch. As we walked down the hallway, we noticed that two teachers were engaged in a rather heated argument in front of the copy machine. Pat, my teacher's aide, and I noticed that all twenty-three of our students had also witnessed the event. I figured that the students would want to talk about it after lunch, and talk about it, they did!

The students came back from lunch upset about the argument. "Did you see those teachers in a fight, Ms. Brown? They weren't showing good character!" I knew that I needed to address this matter in a professional way. "Without talking about the specific teachers involved," I said, "let's talk about ways that we can resolve conflict peacefully." Then we had a five-minute discussion on the subject.

Later that afternoon, I took the students outside for recess. A few minutes later there was a problem over by the swings. Two little girls who usually got along well with each other were tugging and fighting over a swing. I watched to see if they would be able to resolve the conflict on their own. But as the disagreement escalated, I walked toward them. Before I could intervene, a young student appeared on the scene. She put one hand on her hip and pointed a finger in the faces of the squabbling students. "Stop arguing," she directed, "you're starting to act like the teachers around here!"

Lesson learned? Students are always watching. That is one small point we all need to remember every day!

18 Take Five!

Five minutes doesn't seem like very much time, but if well used, it can make a huge difference in the life of a child. Taking five minutes with a student, one on one, is a powerful catalyst for making a child feel loved and valued. And when students can sense our sincere interest in them, they take on the wings of achievement.

So find some time in your day to connect with your students. I sometimes go into the cafeteria and find a student who is finished eating breakfast or lunch and invite that student to the classroom to help with a task. While working together, we share conversation that helps the human element of teaching come alive. Students feel valued and needed, and the closeness gives them a special bond to their school environment. While the main purpose of the invitation is the conversation, kids feel they are helping their teacher and their school by performing the classroom chore. By giving, they receive much more, and the extra attention from a teacher helps develop the self-respect and confidence necessary for all learning.

19 The Locker Room Chat

Just like a team that is pulled into the locker room at half time of the big game, a teacher can pull his class into the locker room for a mid-game pep talk. I have found that a locker room chat is needed about every two weeks to help keep students on track.

When the need arises, I just stop whatever we are working on and say, "Half-time!" Students stop and listen as the coach interjects a motivational message. This can be very helpful when you notice a slip in student attention to task, when students aren't doing their homework, are acting in a disrespectful manner, or are causing disruptions to get your attention. Whenever you notice one of these "culprits" robbing your students of the opportunity to achieve excellence, take time to talk the players back into the game. Don't wait until the game is over and the losing score is flashing on the scoreboard. Just jump right in and signal half time! A locker room chat can get your team back on track with a winning score!

20 Step Up to the Plate!

Encouraging students to step up to the plate is a grand ambition! Just like the baseball player who steps up to the plate during his turn at bat, students need to step up and accept responsibility for their learning. When I see students trying to slip through the cracks, I remind them to step up to the plate, instead.

Many times during the school day, students will notice that someone or something is in need. It could be another classmate or a staff member. Or it could be a task that needs attention. A responsible student will step up to the plate and assume the responsibility for taking care of that need. When you see this happen, praise and celebrate that student! It will give other students the motivation and modeling necessary to help them to step up when it's their turn at bat!

21 The Common Good

Developing character is an individual goal. There is no magic wand. It takes work! We need to be reflective about the kinds of changes we need to make in ourselves in order to be the best person and student that we can be. But part of that journey is the fact that we also need to contribute to the common good.

Aristotle taught that the only way to be happy in life is to be good. How true! He taught about intellectual virtue and moral virtue. His teachings inspire us to use *our* good to create a *common* good. It's a great lesson for all of us. Students and teachers need to contribute to the common good of their school, community, and country. It's an insightful and meaningful way to teach patriotism and good citizenship!

22 Gratitude Journals

Years ago, one of my teaching colleagues saw a segment on *Oprah* on the power of writing each day in a Gratitude Journal. Kathi, my colleague, told me about it and we both were sold on the idea. She and I are now teaching different levels at different schools, so our "takes" on the idea are a little different. The important thing is not *how* you do them, but *that* you do them!

Every year for a Christmas gift, I go to the Dollar Store and buy a blank journal for each of my students. I make and laminate an inscription, and I glue it inside the book's front cover.

On the first day after they open their gifts, I model some ideas for writing by sharing some of the entries I have written in my own journal. I also share some of the wonderful entries that former students have written. Then I give them class time for thinking and writing. Each day right after lunch is the time that seems to work best. I have found that if I expect it to be done outside of class, students forget or put it off. But these small deposits of class time have paid big dividends in student attitude and behavior. This writing exercise has also gone a long way in helping my students develop their writing skills. Here a few entries from young Caitlyn, one of my kindergarten students.

> This Gratitude Journal is given with the hope that you will take the time each day to write down several things that you are thankful for. This will help you to become reflective about your life...and to see things in a more positive light. It will also help you develop the happiness habit. Look for the good in life. I trust that you will find it!
>
> I love you very much!
>
> Ms. Brown

"I am glad that the sun finally came out!" *(And after more than a week of gray winter skies, I'm glad, too!)*

"I'm thankful for kids who keep our school clean!"

"I like my new haircut."

It is easy to see that Caitlyn is developing the happiness habit by learning to look for the best in life. Now treat yourself to some writings from twelve-year-old Drew, who had just moved to West Virginia from Florida. As you will see, Drew is quite a writer. He is a deep thinker, as well, busy developing the "attitude of gratitude" that is part of the character ethic.

"Today the rooftops and the cars are covered with snow from last night. That's what I am thankful for." (*Can you sense Drew's excitement at seeing his very first snow?*)

"Today I learned that teamwork is the best work of all. It helps get work done faster, and it's fun working with your friends. So I would rather choose teamwork than any work."

"I am thankful for my friends because we can talk to them when we need to."

"I am thankful for the blue color in the sea and the amazing starfish and jellyfish that you don't see every day. And the sound of the waves splashing against the water, and the seagulls. The sounds of them make me calm." (*As you can probably guess, Drew's love of the seashore is something I can really understand and relate to!*)

"I am thankful for girls because we can get a girlfriend when we need one!"

The best way to guard against writer's block is to ask your students each week if anyone would like to share his journal entry. Some students love to read them aloud. Their ideas will help the other students think of things that are important to them. I never force anyone to share an entry. Encouragement is always the best path!

23 Service to Others

Good deeds are a natural outgrowth of character teaching. It is not enough to *learn* the character message. The next step is to *live* it! For homework each weekend I give four standard assignments. Each Friday it is the same. Students write the assignment in their assignment notebooks.

- Read for twenty minutes each day.
- Spend time with your family.
- Do a good deed.
- Have fun!

I can't think of a better way to end the week. It might sound like fluff, but my students take this assignment seriously. During our morning meeting the following Monday, I check to see how they spent their time. Good deeds are recorded on a classroom chart. I simply take a large 12 x 18-inch piece of colored construction paper, label it *Good Deeds* or *Service To Others*, laminate it and post it in the classroom. On Monday, or any time a good deed is performed, the student takes a computer sticky label out of a nearby basket. He records his name, the date and a description of the service performed. He then peels the backing from the label and sticks it on the chart. It only takes a moment to write up. And before the school year is over, we have charts all over the classroom! This activity creates a wonderful awareness and serves as motivation to be of service to others.

"The only ones of you who will be truly happy are those who have sought out and found how to serve."

—Albert Einstein

24 An Important Step Back!

Thinking back to a special kindergarten year, I remember when service learning took on a whole different meaning. The students decided on their own that they would start a Book Club. It was not in my lesson plans, but a natural outcome of the writing opportunities provided in the classroom. The students asked me for time each day for their club meetings. I agreed and they set to work. Over a three-and-a-half-week period, they wrote and illustrated thirty-seven little eight-page, stapled-together books, then asked for a basket in which to keep them.

One day after being absent from school, I noticed that the book basket was empty. Two days later, the children came in and dumped change from their pockets onto the classroom tables. I asked where they had gotten their money. "We sold our books," they told me. "You *what*?" I asked in disbelief. "We sold our books!" they responded with pride.

My students had gone out into their neighborhoods, pulling wagons filled with books. Knocking on doors, they offered to read a story for free. And at the end of the story—and who could resist—the neighbor could buy the book.

Their efforts had raised $7.81. I asked what they planned to do with the pennies, nickels, and dimes. The kids said that if I would let them have their Book Club meeting right then, they would decide and let me know. I took that important step back. The Book Club members decided that they wanted to give the money to the poor. It took some time, but together we wrote a letter, which we sent to an organization in our town that feeds the poor through a community lunch program. My students received a letter back from the director thanking them. I made copies, and the kindergarten kids took them home that day to show their parents.

The next year, their first-grade teacher told me that my students had respectfully informed her that they *would be having* the Book Club again in first grade. They didn't ask. They didn't demand. They just had high expectations! These were kids on a mission, kids of conviction, kids of character! So the moral of the story is this: Take lots of steps back and occasionally let your students lead the way. The results can be heartwarming.

25 Service Learning

Taking the idea of service learning into the entire community is a grand idea. Many high schools now offer a class in Community Service Learning. Our high school does and it is wonderful to have service-learning students visit our elementary school each day. First, it gives younger students an opportunity to get to know older kids. They engage in good discussions and dialogue and begin to develop healthy relationships with these high school students. It is good for the high school kids to think about and plan for being good role models. And a service-learning program is helpful to the teacher! I certainly appreciate the classroom chores accomplished by my service-learning student. I enjoy working with the older students, and I think it is important that I provide a good example and mentoring experience for them.

Another activity directly related to service learning is the peer-tutoring program at our school. My sixth-grade class is paired with a first-grade class. Each week the buddies get together for thirty minutes. The sixth graders help the younger students with their spelling words for the week, read stories to them, help with special projects, talk, and just have fun. This program has done a great deal to help build a positive climate in our classroom and our school. We've seen that as students grow in character, the academic skills they practiced together help ensure mastery!

26 Kid Lessons In Character

This is one of my very favorite ideas. I came up with it seven years ago when I was writing my first book, *Lessons From The Rocking Chair: Timeless Stories For Teaching Character.* In that book, I recalled the wisdom I was raised on. My great-grandmother, Maw Great, would sit in her rocking chair reading me stories. At the end of each story there would always be a moral lesson. *"And the moral of the story is...,"* she would say. I could never get enough of her rocking-chair wisdom! So, I took the time to write down as many of those lessons as I could remember.

> ### Rocking Chair Wisdom
> • **Pretty is as pretty does.**
> • **Don't do what's easy, do what's right.**
> • **Honesty is the best policy.**
> • **Hard work never hurt anyone.**
> • **You're judged by the company that you keep.**
> • **Actions speak louder than words.**
> • **Be accountable for your words and deeds.**
> • **Just be yourself.**
> • **Follow your heart.**

I use this timeless wisdom in my own classroom. The repetition of these lessons helps students internalize and live out the character message. It also helps them to think about and recognize their own ideas about good living. To record their thoughts and share them with others, I hung a large pocket chart on my wall titled *Kid Lessons In Character.* The chart started off empty the first day of school. In preparation for the activity, I simply cut white construction paper into three-inch squares—the size of the pockets on the chart. Students were free to do this activity in their free time or at home, as it is a supplement to the instructional day. As students think of good character lessons or tidbits of wisdom, they take the precut paper from the basket and write their name in ink on the bottom and their words of wisdom at the top. In the middle, they draw a colorful picture to illustrate their idea. I always model for them by doing the first one to display in the pocket chart.

The enthusiasm of the students is contagious! It takes about half of the school year to fill the sixty-six pockets in the chart. They love having their ideas on display in the classroom. It's a great teaching tool and a great morale builder.

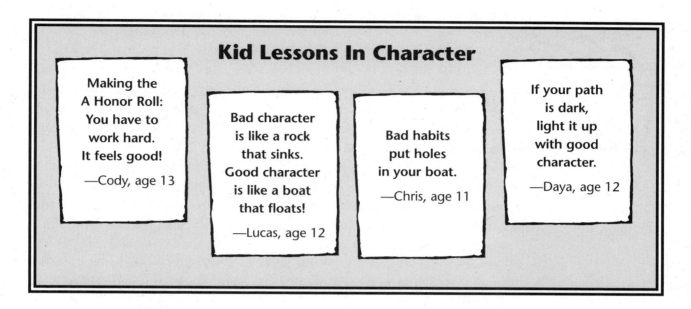

Kid Lessons In Character

Making the
A Honor Roll:
You have to
work hard.
It feels good!

—Cody, age 13

Bad character
is like a rock
that sinks.
Good character
is like a boat
that floats!

—Lucas, age 12

Bad habits
put holes
in your boat.

—Chris, age 11

If your path
is dark,
light it up
with good
character.

—Daya, age 12

27 "Repeat After Me!"

Now that you have collected so much wonderful wisdom, get ready to use it! This is an opportunity to make a big difference in the character development of your students without spending money or time. Sounds too good to be true, doesn't it?

Several times throughout the school day I will say, "Repeat after me!" And then I will select a character axiom for intentional reinforcement. I use only one each day, such as: *Be in the right place, at the right time, doing the right thing!* I say the axiom once, and the students repeat it one time. I might start the day with this activity. Later on, I may use this exercise when we are lining up to go to the library or physical education class. The opportunity may arise again as we line up to go to lunch, the restroom, or our lockers. The final opportunity may arrive when as students pack their backpacks at the end of the school day.

Without taking any time out of our instructional day, we have repeated our tidbit of wisdom five or six times. Meanwhile, the students have it committed to memory. No cost is involved, just the commitment to do this each and every day. I have beamed with joy when overhearing students in our school repeating these nuggets of wisdom to each other. Hopefully, they will internalize the character messages and use them in their lives. This is another small thing that reaps big rewards!

28 Recycling Project

I'm a writer, so I use lots of paper. And I love trees. So it really bothers me to just throw away paper scraps. This is why I recycle. When I transferred to my new school, I found that a recycling program was not in place. But as a personal choice, I kept a recycling bin in my classroom and encouraged students to recycle. Every Friday I would gather up the used paper and take it to the home of a friend, Linda. She lives in the city limits where they pick up items for recycling each Monday. Linda was very kind to let me bring my home and school recycling bags to her house each week. At school, I tried to get some of the other teachers interested in recycling. It was slow going at first. Then I took an important step back and let the kids spread the message. It worked!

When children see the need for something and feel that it is important, their enthusiasm becomes contagious. Just put them in charge of the project, and the rest will be history! I selected several students to go to each classroom in the school and gather the recycling. At first there was none, but when teachers knew that it would be collected, they came on board. I got some recycling bins for the classrooms and we were off! We called the city recycling office and arranged for the paper to be picked up at our school. Recycling Day at our school is on Thursday, so each Wednesday afternoon we start collecting. At the end of the day, the recycling team takes large garbage bags around to the classrooms to collect the used paper. The kids love doing this!

During the first months of our recycling campaign, we gathered about seven large bags of used paper each week. Now, more classrooms are involved and we are collecting eighteen to twenty bags each week for the city recycling truck to pick up. Recycling is a wonderful way to show our respect as good citizens of the earth. And the lessons taught to kids by the example of this caring are invaluable in building character.

29 Marquee Messages

In front of our school stands the school marquee. At Weimer Elementary School, the marquee was the responsibility of a parent and it was used to announce important school events. One day, the parent volunteer asked if my class could take over the responsibility. I was thrilled to accept! I saw it as a great opportunity to share our character message with our community. On one side of the marquee, we listed the important coming events. On the other side, we displayed a character message. People driving to and from our community can see both sides. The results have been magical!

Our principal has received phone calls from members of the community complimenting our school on the positive messages. Many parents have stopped by the principal's office to give a thumbs-up of approval. And the students are now actually *reading* the marquee. From time to time, they even see their own character wisdom on display. It was a small change, but one with a big impact on school climate. Our school is sending the message out into the community that we expect good things. In fact, we expect excellence! We are working hard to build good students and good people. I know that you are, too. Here are a few marquee messages to help get you started.

- **Our goal is personal and academic excellence!**
- **Don't do what's easy...do what's right!**
- **For a child, love is spelled T-I-M-E.**
- **Character and academics taught here!**
- **No one slips through the cracks in this school!**
- **We appreciate supportive parents like you!**
- **Teamwork in any community is always the best work!**
- **Words can build up or tear down. Choose your words wisely!**
- **We believe! We achieve! We succeed!**
- **Teaching character changes things because it changes people!**
- **Have a safe and fun summer! Grow in goodness!**

---

30 School Newsletters

Another great way to get the character message to parents is to send it home in student backpacks. A classroom or school newsletter is a very common communication tool. Just remember to have a separate *Character In The Classroom* section in your newsletter. It's a great way to let parents know what is going on. Another wonderful addition to the newsletter is to have a separate column that teaches a specific character message. One teacher can author the column for the entire year, or teachers can take turns. This is also a powerful way to teach parents how to teach character to their children!

31 Blue Stars!

Think of your own school days. You worked hard on a paper or a test. You really did your best. But then, when you got your paper back from your teacher, the grade was a 91%. You didn't even notice the 91%. You noticed only the 9% missing from the score. You didn't focus on the good parts of your work. Your focus was on the parts marked up and highlighted with red pencil. In my second year of teaching, I learned to tune in to kids then threw out my red pencils and put a new blue Flair pen in my pocket. It has since become a permanent fixture in my pocket—a part of Deb. I don't mark things *wrong* with my blue pen. I mark things *RIGHT*! I make lots of blue stars around the things that I choose to celebrate. The response from students has been magical! The result? Increased student self-confidence, higher achievement, and a strong desire to learn!

Self-confidence is the foundation of all learning. I believe that our self-confidence is built in direct proportion to the strength and structure of our character. Teaching for character translates academically and must be the beginning of the educational journey we make with our students. In your classroom, take steps to eliminate the negative and accentuate the positive. The result will be a positively wonderful experience!

32 "I'm Proud of You!"

A change of attitude and ink color is not enough. Don't stop there! Take the time to write personal notes of pride and encouragement on each student's paper. It is definitely worth the extra moment that it takes. Write a quick note such as, *I'm proud of you! Way to go! Hard work pays off!* Then draw a heart nearby. This goes a long way in inspiration and motivation for the kids in your life.

33 "Thank You!"

Another extension of this positive practice is to thank students for their hard work and effort. I learned this strategy from master teacher, Charlie Abourjilie, who lives and teaches in North Carolina. Charlie tells of a time when he thanked a student for her hard work and commitment to learning. The student was really touched. It seems that no teacher had ever thanked her before for trying her best, despite the difficult circumstances in her life. Charlie had recognized the deep need in his students to be valued and affirmed. And what is more important, he responded to that need!

Since hearing Charlie tell this story, I have been taking the time to thank my students for their hard work and effort. After a test, at the end of the grading period, or at award assemblies, I extend my hand and my heart and say that powerful word that touches students deeply...*thanks!* Just knowing that a teacher has recognized and appreciated the extra effort helps many students go on to bigger and better achievements!

34 Collecting Schedules

The way that I feel about teaching transcends the classroom to the very community of which it is a part. Issues that inspire me to action are those that involve the self-concept and character of children. Therefore, youth sporting programs are close to my heart. I collect the schedules of my students and try to attend at least one event for each student each school year.

I'll never forget the first time I walked through the gymnasium door and headed for the bleachers to support one of my students. I sat with parents and cheered proudly during the game! Basketball, baseball, football, a music recital, or soccer—the outcome was always the same. The look on my student's face was reward enough. I knew this was a habit I wanted to keep. It proved to them that their teacher cared beyond the school walls, beyond the school day. Just showing up makes the statement, even if I can't stay for the entire game. I have been known to coordinate schedules so I could get to three games within a couple of hours on a Saturday morning. It's not a bad way to start off a weekend...not bad at all!

If students have no schedule to give you, there are other ways to let them know how much you care. I have been known to drive through their neighborhoods and stop when I see them outside in the yard. A few shots at the driveway basketball hoop and a few kind words by the fence speak volumes!

35 The Ladder of Achievement

Years ago, I ran across the Ladder of Achievement, a great visual for teaching students the powerful message of effort and determination. I made a big poster out of it, laminated it and put it on the wall in my classroom. During the school year, I refer to it often and the students do, too. Early in the year, the students replicate the poster in their Character Journals. I am sharing it with you so that you can share it with the students in your life. Hopefully, each student will take steps up the ladder to a more successful future. When students get stuck on a rung of the ladder, it helps them see what the next step can be. This is a great tool that we use often in my classroom. I hope it helps your students climb to new heights!

The Ladder of Achievement
100% means **I did!**
90% means **I will.**
80% means **I can.**
70% means **I think I can.**
60% means **I might.**
50% means **I think I might.**
40% means **I'll think about it.**
30% means **I wish I could.**
20% means **I don't know how.**
10% means **I can't.**
0% means **I won't.**

36 Student of the Week/Month

At our elementary school, each classroom teacher selects a *Student of the Week*. This student receives the award on Friday in front of the student body during lunchtime. At first, the award was given mostly for academic effort and achievement. An added component now is the character part of the award. Being respectful, responsible, and caring is now weighed when considering students for the award. It is a great idea to consider the whole child when giving out awards. To show how far we've come, our school even started giving out Character Awards at our school Social Studies and Science Fair. These awards commend students for effort, work ethic, and teamwork. When you think about it, it really isn't hard to find new ways to celebrate evidence of good character!

37 Zero Heroes

As part of our Responsible Students discipline program, we keep track of the number of rule violations that students accumulate during the school week. At the end of the week, we tally them up. On Monday morning, I have a sign-in sheet ready for those students who broke *zero* rules in the behavior and responsibility categories. The *Zero Heroes* add their signatures to the sheet, and it is posted in the classroom. This gives students recognition for their good decisions and encourages others to try for the honor. We also have a bulletin board just outside the principal's office where we honor the students in our school who were Zero Heroes for the entire month!

38 Our Character Is Shining Through!

This is a take-off on the old idea of *catch 'em doing good!* At Lakewood School, the idea grew out of a need for more orderly lunch lines in the cafeteria. Our solution took care of that problem, plus it helped reinforce the school's character messages. We had the district maintenance workers come and install a HUGE bulletin board on the cafeteria wall and the teachers decorated it with the heading *Our Character Is Shining Through!* We decorated the border with lots of colorful stars.

> **Our character is shining through!**
>
> Name _____
> Grade _____ Teacher _____
>
> Good character shown:
>
>
> Recognized by _____ Date _____
> Relationship to school community _____

Then teachers made and ran off copies of five-by-seven-inch certificates. Each certificate had a place for the person's name being cited for good character. There was a place for the good-deed commendation, a place for the date, and a place where recipients could sign their name. We made those certificates available throughout the school to everyone: parents, students, teachers and staff. Before long, members of our school community were taking notice of good character in action. They were also taking the time to go beyond just noticing to write up the good works of others.

It didn't take long to get that bulletin board filled with certificates of recognition. Since students were busy reading them while waiting in the lunch line, there was less noise and horseplay in the cafeteria. Reading for character during lunch also provided inspiration and motivation for two things: writing up the good deeds of others and acting in a way that would encourage someone to write about you!

After the certificates had been on display for about two weeks, they were taken down and put in the teacher's mailboxes. Teachers then either sent the certificates home with the students who earned them or let the students glue them inside their student portfolios. The older students in your school can adopt this bulletin board as a service-learning project. They do a wonderful job of putting up and taking down the certificates. It frees up teachers to do other tasks and helps the older students feel good about contributing to their school. And when more space is freed up on the bulletin board, students tend to work their way to recognition, which begins the cycle all over again!

39 Celebrating Incremental Successes

At times, there is no one more disheartened and discouraged about poor student behavior than I am. And yet, no one is more proud of good student behavior! One of the best ways to cultivate a character climate is to look for the best in your students. When you do look for the best, you tend to find it! My students are continually making small, but important, steps towards goodness. It is my job to celebrate these incremental successes. I beam with pride when I see a student holding a door for someone. I truly get excited when a first grader runs into my sixth grade classroom and asks, "Ms. Brown, when are we having the next Character Assembly?" I cherish the note from my substitute teacher who wrote,

"Deb, whatever you are doing with this class is working. They are such a great group of students—ready to work, well behaved and polite. I never knew that 6th graders and this age group could be this way (so nice)."

I am thankful for the blessing of that student Matt, who gave his $25 birthday money to a woman at a McDonald's restaurant who had no money for her dinner. I delighted in running into a kindergarten student in the hallway who said (with his front tooth missing), "I know you! You're the one who 'teached' us about good character!" Definitely icing on the character cake!

Instead of always looking ahead at all of the work to be accomplished, take time to see how far you've come. Once in a while, you will get a glimpse into the impact and power of your teaching. Cherish each of those precious moments. Look for the best in your students. Trust that you will find it!

40 Kindness Counts!

Problems can arise among and within the staff of the school. I remember a time when the cooks in our school were having a difficult time being cheerful. When the kindergarten students went through the cafeteria line, they noticed the change. After a few days of being exposed to the tension, the students asked if they could eat lunch in the classroom. They did not want to go into that lunchroom.

I knew that I could not talk to the students about fellow employees, nor could I go to the cooks with our concern. But what I *could* do was plant some seeds of kindness with my students. So I asked them, "How many of you understand what a tough job the cooks have? They have to get up early every school day and come to school and cook your breakfast. They also have to cook your lunch. Each and every school day, they cook breakfast and lunch for 350 students and 40 staff members. That's almost 800 meals a day. They stand on their feet all day long in a hot kitchen. Do you think that there might be something that *we* can do to cheer them up? Let's try to say or do something each day that will make the cooks glad that we came through their lunch line."

Seeds planted, we went on to lunch. The first student through the line looked up, smiled at the cooks and said, "Thank you." The cooks didn't even notice. The next student said politely, "Oh, you're having macaroni and cheese today. That's my favorite!" Still no smile in sight from the kitchen staff. Then five-year-old Sam came through the line. He is a great kid and also friendly, outgoing, creative, and funny. "Hey there, Cupcake! You're looking good in that pink sweater!" he said. "How about giving me a little extra pudding today?" Well, as you can imagine, smiles finally broke out on the faces of the cooks. Big smiles. In fact, we even heard laughter!

From that day on, the cooks couldn't wait for our class to walk through the line. They began listening to and enjoying the kind words from the students. They also couldn't wait to see what Sam would say next. One day when we were going on a field trip and would not be eating lunch at school, one of the cooks came into our classroom and said, "Have a fun day, kids. We'll miss you at lunch!"

Need I say more? The character message had changed things. The power of the character message is that it *changes things* because it *changes people!* Now get busy planting the seeds of kindness with your students. It will yield a bountiful harvest.

41 The Character Class

Never underestimate the importance of teaching the character message to the whole school at the same time. There is power in numbers. Just as I taught the Character Class at Lakewood my last year there, I kept my promise to my students, and brought the Character Class idea to my new school, Weimer Elementary.

At Weimer, the class had to be taught differently, because it was a different type of school. Situated in the area of town often referred to as "The Badlands," I was careful to build a foundation for learning. The class was held on the last day of the school month and students in grades 1-6 attended. A larger number of students began attending, so the class was usually split into two half-hour sessions. Grades 1-3 attended the first session and grades 4-6 attended the second session. Classroom management was more difficult, so a colleague was on hand to help. As the year went on, teaching the class became more difficult because we were dealing with so many troubled children. This dictated the need for smaller classes, plus a more personal approach. Finally, the school staff decided to alter the game plan. Rather than me teaching every student each month, I began preparing the lessons for the class, which were then taught by the grade-level teachers.

> As a teacher and as a staff, you will need to honor your commitment by moving from incidental to more intentional methods of teaching the character message.
> Then the message will take root through the commitment of your school community.

I will have to admit that I miss teaching the larger Character Class. I miss the interaction with all of the students in the school. But it was time to move on to a different way of doing things so that the needs of our students could be met by all of us. The wonderful thing about the Character Class now is that all of the teachers are teaching it! I see great value in that approach. And with all of us teaching the same lessons during that particular time slot, there is still a sense of school unity.

The important thing is not *how* you teach the class. The important thing is *that* you teach it. Years ago, Dr. William Mitchell from The Power of Positive Students International Foundation, taught me the difference between interest and commitment. For a character initiative to be successful there must be a commitment on the part of the school staff. "Are you *interested* in teaching for character, or are you *committed* to it?" he would ask. As a teacher and as a staff, you will need to honor your commitment by moving from *incidental* to more *intentional* methods of teaching the character message. Then the message will take root through the commitment of your school community.

42 Character Cards

Where do you start? By tuning in to your students, you will find just what you need to do to begin. Kids know what they need. Pay attention, and they will tell you. Look past what they do and look for the reasons *why*. Watch and listen. Listen and watch. For example, building a common language of character at Lakewood grew out of my frustration at trying to find a way to teach my students about a good work ethic. After days and days of incomplete and unacceptable assignments, I was exasperated. That's when I came up with the idea of using the woodpecker to teach the lesson *Keep pecking away!* That was our very first Character Card.

As the school year went on, I watched for more real-life character messages that could teach students the important character lessons that would help them in school. We came up with quite a few. As with the first idea, I made a class poster with each picture and message. I laminated the nine-by-twelve-inch cards and used them every day for reviewing our own personal language of character. For the language to work it must be clear, common, and consistent. When character language was used in my classroom, *good* things began to happen. Then, when our entire school began using character language, even better things appeared on the horizon! Here's my list to help get you started. As the school year goes on, you and your students will have fun adding to the list!

Real-Life Character Messages
(Visuals help students keep their eye on the message!)

Light Bulb: Think about good character!

Exclamation Mark: Get excited about doing the right thing!

Woodpecker: Keep pecking away!

Picture Frame: Picture it! Picture yourself as a kid of character!

Magic Wand: There's no magic wand to acquiring good character. It takes work!

Building Blocks (A+B=C): Attitude + Behavior = Character

Mirror: Look for the best in others...and in yourself!

Star: Get the character habit! It will keep you in the company of stars!

Chalkboard and Eraser: Each day is a clean slate!

Toolbox: Stock your toolbox! (Stock it with good habits!)

Ruler and Yardstick: Measure up! (Measure up to your true potential!)

Doorknob: Run through open doors (of opportunity)!

Pencil: Write down your goals!

Basketball Net: Keep your eye on the goal!

Barbell: Pump yourself up with good character! (Strength training)

Target: Target practice helps!

Candle: Let your character shine through!

Sunglasses: Good character is so bright...you'll need shades!

Broom: If we all sweep in front of our own doors, the whole school will be clean!

43 Character Assemblies

A favorite and fun character-building activity is to hold school-wide Character Assemblies. At Lakewood, I held four during the school year. At Weimer, I put on eight. After I sponsored the assemblies the first year, the Weimer teachers took turns doing them the following years. The students loved these assemblies! They looked forward to them and many students would stop me in the hallway to ask when the next one was scheduled. These assemblies brought a new excitement to Weimer, and I loved putting them together and putting them on!

To help with the planning, I involved my sixth-grade students. The kids had splendid ideas and were eager to help. We decided on a format. Each month we would teach a new character message. The neat thing was that everyone in the school got the message at the same time. Parents, teachers, staff, and students all came together each month to learn. The first message of the school year was the favorite: *Keep pecking away!* The second lesson was, perhaps, the most important: *There is no magic wand to developing good character. It takes work!*

> Research shows that retention of knowledge is 800% higher when you're having fun while you're learning!

The next part of the assembly focused on reviewing The Six Pillars of Character: respect, trustworthiness, responsibility, caring, fairness and citizenship. Then came a song, a poem and a skit. We started the assembly with music and we ended the very same way. It was a high-energy, fun, exciting twenty-five minutes! Research tells us that children and adults learn up to 800% *more* when they are having fun and enjoying themselves while they are learning. So, when you think about the research, we were right on target with these assemblies! Everyone came into the assemblies smiling and left energized.

The real magic happened after the assemblies were over. You could see it in the hallways of school. You could see it in the cafeteria. You could witness it in the classrooms. Students were talking about the assemblies and using the common language and discussing the character messages. They were talking about how the character lessons were helping them in school. When I walked by and heard one of these conversations, I walked the rest of the way down the hallway on air!

The main point of the assembly is to come together as a school to learn about and celebrate good character. It really doesn't matter what you do once you gather together. The format of the assembly is not important. There are as many ideas for these assemblies as there are teachers and students planning them. Just make the lessons fun and enjoyable. You can use songs, stories, skits, poetry and choral readings. They can follow the same familiar format or they can be different every month. Make the time together a real celebration of academics and character. I can promise you some exciting and rewarding moments!

44 Parent-Teacher Thought-Sharing Notebooks

This is an idea from 1991. When our school started a new whole-language approach to learning, we began teaching integrated thematic units. To monitor the struggles and successes of the students, I initiated the use of Parent-Teacher Thought-Sharing Notebooks. It was deeply satisfying to read the entries of the parents and to help chart the success of the program by reading about the personal journeys of the students. This project helped me see the trouble spots and make adjustments in my efforts.

Just last year I thought about those old notebooks and decided to use the same strategy for character education. It was best to start slowly and not bite off more than I could chew, so I began with two parents. I bought two composition books. During the first month of school, I jotted down observations and thoughts about the character education efforts in my classroom. I wrote about specific instances, but was careful not to comment about specific students. Confidentiality is an important professional consideration.

At the beginning of the second month of school, I sent the notebooks home to the parents who had agreed to journal with me on the project. For the next month, the parents recorded their ideas, suggestions, observations, comments, insights, and thoughts about the changes in their children, by simply writing down the date and some personal comments. Over time I have found that some parents will write a little bit each week during the time that they have the notebook, while others will wait until the notebook is due back and will begin summarizing their comments from the month. Favorite comments from my parents have included:

I've noticed that I don't have to fuss at my child about getting started on his homework. He's taking the initiative to get started on his own.

My son is now putting his dirty clothes in the hamper, rather than the usual place—under his bed!

At first I thought that teaching this character stuff was my job and not yours. Now I can see that we all need to work together.

My child takes that good-deed homework assignment seriously. She loves helping others.

My daughter is now studying more for her spelling tests—and she's doing better!

My child is coming home from school telling me all about the character assemblies. He wants me to come and see the next one.

I've noticed the new messages on the school marquee. My son calls them character quotes. Our family can't wait to see what you will put on there next!

The thought-sharing notebook is documentation of your journey with students. Remember that the goal is for them to become better students and better people. Any ideas to help with that are certainly welcome. By the end of the school year, you will have exchanged the notebook with parents several times, so there will be lots of documentation to review. These notebooks help me to see the small, incremental successes that my students are making. They help me to stay positive and encourage me to try new things whenever progress seems fleeting.

Also keep in mind that parents love to participate. They feel that they are getting to know you better and trust is strengthened. They develop a respect for you as a teacher by reading and commenting on your written thoughts. They come to see that you work hard to teach their children and that their children's success in school and in life are important to you. They also expect and encourage progress from their child. The parent-teacher bond is one of the most rewarding aspects of teaching. And when children know that their teacher and parents are working together, they get the idea that school is important. What is more important, *they* feel valued. Communicating that is always a good thing!

45 Find Another Way

There will be times when things don't seem to be working out, but don't give up. Student attitudes may be less than positive and student achievement may be at an all-time low. There will be days when student apathy seems to be the prevailing mood and other times when your students seem to be making bad decisions about their studies and their behavior. All teachers run into ruts and slumps at some point during the school year. At these times we just need an extra push and motivation to spur us on.

I remember a period during my fifth year of teaching when every day for several days, the third grade teacher spent the entire lunch period complaining that her students were not listening and following directions. Sound familiar? We all have those times. She had been instructing students on the procedure for heading their paper for written assignments. Nilda, the teacher, went on to explain that she wanted their name on the top left line and the date on the right. She then wanted them to skip a line and write the subject title in the middle of that third line. It seemed so simple. But every day when Nilda collected the assignments, very few students had followed her instructions. "I'm into the nagging mode," she said, "and not even that is working."

At the time, I was young and naïve and optimistic. What I lacked in experience, I made up for in enthusiasm. While listening to Nilda's complaint for hopefully the last time, I offered to pitch in. "Don't worry, Nilda," I said. "I will try to help this afternoon."

Now, it is a good thing that Nilda and I were friends. I'm sure she wondered that if she, a veteran teacher, couldn't get students to head their papers correctly, just what was this new, inexperienced teacher going to do? The truth is, I didn't know what I was going to do. But, what I did know was that there must be a better way than nagging. I thought back to three special words that baseball great Satchel Paige once said: *"Find another way."* What powerful wisdom! That's all it took to get me going.

My friend, Chris, taught kindergarten with me that school year and I went to her for help. That afternoon we went to the cafeteria and got some pompoms from the cheerleaders' closet. At 1:10 p.m. that same day, the door to the third grade

"Find another way."
—Satchel Paige

classroom opened. In charged two twenty-nine-year-old cheerleaders. We ran right up to the front of the classroom and began our cheer, "What do you do when you write your name? Skip a line...skip a line! What do you do when you write your name? Skip a line...skip a line! What do you do when you write your name? Skip a line..." Then we paused and waited for the student response.

"SKIP A LINE!" they yelled back in unison. It was a wonderful moment. Chris and I jumped into the air. Then, with our pompoms shaking in the breeze, we ran out of the room just as quickly and enthusiastically as we had run in.

The entire class sat quietly in amazement. I will have to admit that Nilda wasn't quite sure what she had just witnessed. But as I looked back, she *was* smiling. The next day at lunch, Nilda had no complaints. The cheer had worked! The students were remembering, with a smile, to head their papers correctly.

So when you are faced with the challenges of day-to-day teaching and your students challenge you at every turn, remember the words of Satchel Paige and *find another way*. What will be the choice for the students in your life? Will you nag them or cheer them on?

46 The Writing Is on the Wall!

I put all of my important messages on the wall. Right there, up high, near the ceiling, I cut out large colorful letters and laminate them and spell out the following four twelve-foot sentences that are meant to guide:

OUR DECISIONS DEFINE US!

OUR GOAL IS PERSONAL AND ACADEMIC EXCELLENCE!

I THINK I CAN...I KNOW I CAN!

DON'T DO WHAT'S EASY...DO WHAT'S RIGHT!

Four walls, four sentences. The truth of the matter is, I use these walls and teach from them. Whenever a message is needed to drive home the point, I can honestly say that the answer is always close at hand. In fact, the writing is on the wall!

That higher-level wall space is typically wasted anyway. No one ever hangs posters or artwork up so high. These four powerful sentences are now high and mighty reminders of the character lessons that can change your life, if you read them, if you use them, and if you choose to live by them. And the wonderful thing is that kids will take these messages to heart.

47 The Little Triangle in Your Heart

A few summers ago, I was doing some research on character and ran across the following illustration from an unknown author:

Your conscience is like a little triangle in your heart. It acts like a pinwheel.
When you do bad things it spins around, and the corners hurt you a lot.
If you keep on making bad decisions and act on them, the corners wear off.
And when the little triangle spins around again, it doesn't hurt anymore.

Wow! What a great analogy for teaching young children the workings of a good conscience. You can see the power of that little triangle poking you back to the reality of your actions. You can also see the devastating results when the warnings are ignored.

This is a wonderful activity for your students. Each school year I explain the lesson. Then we set to work making our own triangle out of poster board or tag board. The students keep the little triangles in their backpacks or lockers as a reminder of this all-important character lesson. I have been known to spin a few triangles in my day and love the encouragement that this visual provides as I try to be a better person. A little reminder often goes a long way in reinforcing the lesson for your students!

48 Learning Equations

Creating a climate for learning is an important endeavor. There are so many things to consider. Each and every school day is different. No two activities are ever alike. So it is important to remember that there are some basic equations that will produce learning. I remember my first teaching job. The principal took me on a tour of the school and I noticed that all of the student desks were arranged the same way. Long rows of isolated desks lined each classroom. I also noticed that the classrooms were quiet. It led me to believe that the formula for successful learning was: *Quiet + Isolation = Learning*. Gee, did I ever have a lot to learn! And over the years, I did learn. I have made up many subsequent equations that add up to successful learning. After reading my list, take the time to make up a few of your own. This is also a fun and interesting activity to do with students. They will have wonderful ideas to add!

> **Excitement + Interest = Learning**
> **Groups of Students + Discussion = Learning**
> **Exploration + Discovery = Learning**
> **Research + Thinking = Learning**
> **Effort + Hard Work = Learning**

Now, let's change the equation! Let's let the answer to each equation be *good character*. Here are some equations my students in the Character Classes have made up:

> **Good Work Ethic + Effort = Good Grades**
> **Friendship + Caring = A Happy Life**
> **Honesty + Lots of Study Time = Good Test Scores**
> **Responsibility + Hard Work = Skill Mastery**
> **Respect + Kind Words = Happy Parents**
> **Self Respect + Integrity = A Kid of Character**

The possibilities within this activity are endless. Enjoy making equations of your own. It doesn't take a mathematician to figure these out!

49 The Most Important Lesson of the Day

It was April, and the students had spring fever. They were restless and antsy and more than anything wanted to be outside in the sunshine. It was a difficult time to keep students on task. Discontent and restlessness permeated the room. This particular day we were in the middle of Journal Writing. The students were writing, but they were also whispering. Some were even looking out the window. Little did I know how the events of this day would unfold.

All of a sudden Bryan jumped up! He grabbed my sharp teacher scissors from a girl and refused to give them back to her. A scramble broke out at the table. I walked toward the trouble...literally. And what I saw changed me forever. Right there, under my nose, one of the other students had just failed at an attempt to slit her wrist with the school-issue scissors. Thank God they wouldn't cut paper, much less skin! Then she had reached for mine.

The next few minutes were crazy and confusing. But thanks to the character lessons on caring and responsibility, a student had intervened and, perhaps, had saved this girl's life. She had written a suicide note in her journal and then had tried to saw her wrist with those dull school scissors. Unsuccessful at the attempt, she had tried to gain access to a sharper pair.

But Bryan had stepped up to the plate. He had taken responsibility for his classmate. It was one of my proudest moments as a teacher. Character education had saved the day! It had, at the very least, saved a student's life.

Carol, the student who had attempted suicide, had a childhood filled with problems. Thirteen years of them. She was looking for a way out, and those scissors offered her the door that she felt she needed. Later, after sending Carol off to the hospital, I took the time to talk with my students about what had happened. We spent over forty-five minutes discussing adversity, decision-making, and resiliency skills. We talked about how our decisions define us, and how we have to hang on to that moral rope when making decisions. We talked about how the character lessons are more than something we *learn*, that they are something we *live*! It was a difficult and emotional discussion.

At the end of that school day, I collapsed in my teacher's chair, buried my head in my hands and cried. I thanked God for the blessing of His intervention. And I thought about how closely I had come to losing a student. Right there in my classroom. Right under my nose. Right before my very eyes. It was a chilling thought, to say the least.

As I reflected on the day, I thought about all I had taught my students. Earlier in the day I had taught a lesson on multiplying fractions and a lesson on proper nouns. I had also taught a lesson on the difference between fact and opinion and a lesson on prefixes and their meanings. I took time to ask myself a very important question: *Just what was the most important lesson of the day?*

The answer was easy. The most important lesson of the day was the character lesson on resiliency that came after Carol's departure from school. The reason for sharing this painful story? I want you to know that there will be days when the most important lesson in your day will not be academic. But because you have your

moral rope to hang on to and the character lessons tucked under your proverbial belt of wisdom, you will be ready for the challenge. I've taught a lot of lessons in my day, but on this particular day, Carol taught me to look beyond the academics for the most important lesson of all!

50 The 2 and 4 Rule

Teaching students to become responsible *to* each other and *for* each other is a natural outgrowth of teaching for character. I call this the *2 and 4 Rule* of caring and friendship. Whenever I see the need for the rule to be used in our classroom, I just give students the two-finger, then the four-finger signal. It works. Just ask Carol!

51 Student Testimonials

Have you ever head the expression *The greater the test, the greater the testimony*? It is true! Just give your students a chance to prove it and you will be sold on this strategy for life! You've got to wait until the time is right, though. Then, when the opportunity arrives, jump on it with both feet!

I'll never forget that magical time in the classroom. A sixth-grade student, Cody had worked hard all week to master the skills for a test. I mean he really worked hard! His stepmother had helped him each night as he reviewed and studied for the test. By Friday, Cody was confident. When I passed out the test, he set to work. His pencil got quite a workout that day!

When the tests were graded, Cody had earned an A. I couldn't wait to pass the test back the next day. The look on his face when he saw his grade was priceless. I knew we had to share this with his classmates.

I called Cody up front to share his news. "Cody, would you like to give a testimonial?" He couldn't wait! He walked up to the front of the classroom with a smile so big it wouldn't fit on his face. He said simply and powerfully, "Making an A on this test was hard, but it feels good!"

The whole class broke out in spontaneous applause. I couldn't have driven home the point any better. And believe me, Cody's classmates took heart!

52 Just Trust!

It's amazing to see how you can transform a classroom with trust! I think you will find that your students tend to live up to the trust that you place in them. After all, the most important relationship between a teacher and student is trust.

A great way to start off the school year with a new class of children is to tell them that you trust them. Encourage them along the way. When they do make mistakes or betray your trust, use the situation as a teaching experience to move them back onto the honesty track. And always remember that modeling trust is the most important part of the plan!

The greater the test, the greater the testimony.

Ways that you can *show* trust become ways that you can *cultivate* trust in your kids:

> • **Have high expectations for every student.**
>
> • **Place extra responsibility on them.**
>
> • **Sometimes let them grade their own assignments and quizzes.**
>
> • **Ask them to run an errand or help another student.**
>
> • **Let them assume classroom chores that you usually do.**
>
> • **Give them opportunities to rise to the occasion of honesty.**
>
> • **Give them a precious gift...the benefit of the doubt!**

53 Expect the Best!

It's a self-fulfilling prophecy. When you expect the best from your students, you most often get it! Most students respond to the invitation of personal and academic growth. Generally, all kids *want* to be good! I believe that students will likely live up to your expectations of them. Remember that criticism and pejorative remarks tend to breed an atmosphere of mistrust and mediocrity. But the good news is that encouragement, praise, motivation, and inspiration weave a fabric of success!

So when deciding on the expectations for your class, expect the best!

54 Attention/Detention

Students have two choices in school and in life. They can choose to draw attention to themselves with good choices in academics and behavior. Or they can choose to draw detention with their poor choices. The positive attention for good study skills and good behavior comes in the form of good report cards, honor roll achievement, and a reputation for good behavior. The detention that is earned with bad behavior and lack of effort often comes in the form of a trip to the principal's office. Whenever I see students ready to make a bad decision, I remind them of their two options: attention or detention. The choice is up to them!

55 Teaching Seats

I know that this one sounds funny, but it shows that you can make a character lesson out of just about any opportunity. In the principal's office sat seven new chairs, all in a row and all the same color. Mr. Handley, the principal, called me in and said, "Deb, could you make some character posters for the backs of my new chairs? That way, when the kids and parents come in, they will get the message...the character message!"

What a wonderful idea! I set to work. I went back to my classroom and typed up Mr. Handley's seven favorite character quotes and printed them out on brightly colored paper. Then I went to the workroom and laminated them. Then I adhered a character poster to the back of each chair.

I have to admit that the posters really spruced up his office. More important, they gave everyone who visited a starting place for conversation about the mission of our school. Many times, the principal would ask a student who had been sent to the office to select the appropriate chair to sit in. He would then let the child think about things for a minute before they started talking.

Kids, parents, and teachers all came to love the messages on those chairs. Here are the seven character messages that we used. Have fun thinking of more!

- **You can't talk your way out of something that you've already behaved your way into!**
- **A bad attitude is like a flat tire. You can't go anywhere until you change it!**
- **No matter how far you've gone down a wrong road, turn back!**
- **You don't have to attend every argument that you're invited to!**
- **Don't do what's easy...do what's right!**
- **When things go wrong, don't go with them!**
- **Just tell the truth. It will save you every time!**

56 A Moral Rope

Once, when I was going through a difficult time, a friend said, "Deb, when you get to the end of your rope, tie a knot and hang on." It was a welcome lesson in perseverance. Those inspiring words are attributed to President Franklin D. Roosevelt. He was a seasoned veteran in courage and determination.

I believe that character teaching and training gives kids a *moral rope* to hang on to during the decision times of childhood and beyond. That moral rope will give them the support they need to choose *right* in the decisions facing them. Sometimes we need to hang on just a little longer until we find the strength we need. Teaching for character is that support. It provides that moral rope.

I have a piece of rope that I carry with me. Years ago, I cut it from a lobster trap at the beach. At both ends of the rope, I tied a knot. It's a great reminder of the lessons that have helped me grow strong. There are always times when the support and reinforcement of that rope is needed and appreciated. And so, each year I give one to my students as a gift. I bring a long rope clothes line to school, about half-an-inch in diameter. We each cut off a piece and tie a knot at each end. The students walk away with their moral rope as a souvenir of our year together learning about character. But we all know that they have taken away much more.

57 The Class Song

Every school year, we use a myriad of songs during class arrival time, dismissal time, and for special projects and assemblies. And with each school year, a class favorite naturally emerges. I can honestly say that has happened each of the last fifteen years. Hearing that song later on helps bring back many fond memories from your year with the kids. When you hear the song, it is like playing a home movie of memories in your mind.

Remember, too, that songs are powerful links to the past. Having a class song will help your students remember their year, long after they have left your classroom. Choose songs with good lyrics for helping them remember the lessons that you have tried to teach. Academic lessons and character lessons will be remembered by all when they hear your class song!

58 Student Surveys

If you want to really know what the kids think, just ask! At the end of the school year I use students surveys to find out about the year and what they learned. The surveys include several questions about our character education effort. Below are some of my favorite responses from over the years. Read on and smile!

What did you like about the Character Class?

- Learning character in fun activities
- It taught me right from wrong.
- That everyone was behaving
- That we could do lots of the talking

What were your favorite character lessons?

- Keep pecking away!
- Caring, trustworthiness, citizenship, and respect
- Learning about the six "caterpillars" of character
- Do the right thing!
- Always do your best!
- Keep your eye on the goal!

What are some of your new goals?

- To be a good person
- To do all of my homework
- To never give up on anything
- To treat people like they want to be treated
- Not throwing a temper tantrum
- To set a better example

How have the character lessons changed your life?

- They made me believe in myself.
- I'm a little bit nicer now.
- I learned not to be violent or mean.
- Now I make the right choices.
- I do my homework.
- I pick up litter.
- I hardly ever get in trouble.
- I learned that you have to give up something to get good grades.
- I'm nicer to people now, and I've got a life!
- It gave me the keys to "secess" (but unfortunately not the key to spelling!).
- I was good and I got "gooder"!

59 Rocks!

In March 1998, I made my first trip to Cortland, New York. I had planned this trip so that I could visit and learn from Dr. Thomas Lickona, who wrote *the book* on character education, *Educating for Character*. Tom was conducting his spring character conference during my visit. It is a follow-up to his widely popular Summer Institute in Character Education. I mailed him a copy of my first book, *Lessons From The Rocking Chair*, as a way of saying thanks for his kind acceptance of my request to visit.

> I still have that special little rock. In fact, I take that rock with me wherever I go to carry the character message.

A few weeks later, Dr. Lickona called me at home, and said, "Deb, I was wondering if you would speak at the conference luncheon." I couldn't believe the words I was hearing. "Gee, Dr. Lickona, I don't know," I said. "How would you even know if you would want me to speak? We haven't even met yet."

Tom responded simply, "I read your book."

It was amazing to me that Tom Lickona had taken the time to read my book. I felt humbled. Tom went on to dangle a carrot in front of me, "Deb, it won't cost you any money to attend the conference if you speak. We'll call it an even exchange." Now, this trip wasn't costing me any money, as my school district would be paying for my travel to New York. Even so, I accepted the opportunity to save them money and said yes to Tom's kind and generous offer.

Just days before I was to leave for New York, I received news that my teaching position would be cut at Lakewood School. I was devastated. I had taught at Lakewood for twelve years. Nineteen teachers had transferred to Lakewood since I had been there and only four teachers had been there longer than I. But being low man on the proverbial totem pole of seniority was the deciding factor. I would be the teacher losing her job.

I went to New York on March 26 and spent three wonderful days learning from the master. I spent time in Tom's office reading from his extensive collection of books. I spent an evening with him observing his graduate class. Tom even found time to have dinner with me. It was an incredible trip!

On the day of the conference, I got up to speak at lunch. I walked to the microphone and felt the awesome importance of that day. I prefaced my luncheon remarks by saying what I always say, "I am not an expert in the field." Just then a voice from the middle of the ballroom called out, "If you aren't an expert, who is?" I looked up to see that it was Tom who had made the remark. Now you've got to understand my predicament. Speaking about character education in front of Tom Lickona would be like speaking about Christianity with Jesus in the audience. He knows his stuff!

The room fell silent. I responded to Tom's well-intentioned question. "You are!" was my honest response. Everyone in the room broke into laughter. It eased my tensions and I went on with my talk. After I spoke, there was warm applause. I have to admit that this humble character messenger felt very good inside. I felt that my character message was accepted and I felt valued.

After the presentation, I walked outside and sat on a bench, looking out over the beautiful Cortland campus. I wanted to savor each and every moment of that glorious day. Then I remembered. As I thought about home and the loss of my teaching position, I was overcome with emotion and started to cry. Then I looked down and noticed a small rock on the sidewalk. I picked up that rock and drew a big "X" on the sidewalk. I stood on that "X" and said out loud, as I do when something is really important, "Deb Brown, the rest of your life starts here." And putting one foot in front of the other, I walked off into an unknown future.

That was March 27, 1998. I still have that special little rock. In fact, I take that rock with me wherever I go to carry the character message and always tell that heartfelt story.

In some public schools in America, teachers teach the 3 Rs: reading, 'riting, and 'rithmetic. But character educators always teach the 5Rs: reading, 'riting, 'rithmetic, respect, and responsibility. And now, after reading this book, you have learned about the 7Rs! You have *The Deb Brown Version of American Education*: reading, 'riting, 'rithmetic, respect, responsibility, ropes, and rocks!

Remember that the rest of your life starts here, with the reading of this book. When you finish, stand on the newly drawn "X" in your life. Put one foot in front of the other and walk off into *your* future. With the new ideas you've gathered here, you should be ready to call each of your students to personal and academic excellence with the character message. I wish you a wonderful journey!

Chapter Eight

Building Curriculum

60 The Character Standard

As a teacher, you have high expectations for your students. You love them and want to be sure that none slip through the cracks. An important strategy is to show your students those high expectations and to weave them into the life of your classroom. I call it the *Character Standard*. It is the highest expectation for students, the highest calling.

By calling your students to personal and academic excellence, they will come to realize more of their true potential. The Character Standard will remind them of all that they can be and all that they can become! Students will learn to challenge themselves to do their best. They will begin their travels on the road from mediocrity to excellence. Once they have had a taste of excellence and the intrinsic reward that it brings, they will work even harder to achieve the character standard!

By holding your students to high expectations, you will naturally refuse to accept anything except their *best*. Students will come to respect you for the fact that you accept no late assignments, no unexcused absences or tardies, and no excuses for substandard work and behavior. If a paper is messy and unfinished, you do not even take the time to grade it. When students come in late for class without a reason, they do not get the opportunity to make up missing assignments. When students neglect to do homework, you simply record a zero in the grade book.

These responses must be consistent for each and every student, each and every day of the school year. Then it becomes a fair practice that encourages excellence. When students know that they cannot make excuses in your classroom, they will

> "The classroom is structured so that certain things are likely to occur."
>
> —**Dorothy Strickland**

come to accept the challenge of personal as well as academic growth. They will feel better about their effort, and their self-respect will soar. Then the sky really will be the limit.

61 Defining Character

Creating an awareness of the many good character traits that we can develop in life is always a wonderful first step! But we cannot always assume that our students know what each of these traits mean or how they can be exemplified in their lives. That is where intentional teaching comes into play.

One strategy that works well is to have students go on the prowl for the definitions of these words. They can look the words up in the dictionary, study the lives of famous people who exemplify these traits, ask their family and friends what the words mean to them and watch for the traits lived out in their everyday environment.

> The Egyptian use of the word character means "to shape, to form, to build."

Once the research is done, the next step is to give the matter some serious thought and study. I always tell my students that *studying* means to *read*, *research* and *think* in order to *learn*. Reflection is almost a lost art in today's world. The same might be said for thinking. Many students take the easy way out. They look for shortcuts in regard to their studies and the result is a substandard education. Very rarely do students realize that they are the only ones getting cheated in the process. It is important to teach children how to study and how to learn. Once they have mastered that, the world really begins to open up for them!

After some thought-time, have your students pick up their pencils and start writing. When their working definitions are complete, have the students bring them to class. Discussions will go a long way in helping them to edit and refine their thinking. And once each student has settled in on his final draft of the definition, encourage him to get to work incorporating that trait into his own character.

Below are some kid-examples that I have collected from students at the elementary school level.

RESPECT	• treating others the way I would like to be treated • showing kindness at every turn • letting people's feelings count
TRUSTWORTHINESS	• when you are honest • when you tell the whole truth • when you do what you say you will do • when you keep promises
RESPONSIBILITY	• doing your homework all of the time • doing your chores without being asked • taking care of your belongings • taking care of the earth

FAIRNESS	• taking turns
	• sharing with others
	• treating all as equals
CARING	• showing kindness
	• showing respect to everyone
	• being nice, and never cruel
	• saying nice words or none at all
CITIZENSHIP	• letting everyone have a vote
	• taking your duties seriously
	• caring about your country
	• caring about the people in your school
	• reusing and recycling
	• taking care of the earth
ACCOUNTABILITY	• stepping up to the plate
	• saying "I did it" when asked
	• telling the truth about what happened
	• accepting responsibility for mistakes
INTEGRITY	• being able to be trusted
	• showing good character when no one is looking
	• when people can count on you
	• knowing what you stand for

62 Honor Sentences

One of the most important academic considerations is the honor and integrity of the learner. Doing your own work, giving an assignment your best effort and taking responsibility for your studies are all crucial to the development of a good student. In an effort to promote honesty and integrity, I have students write an Honor Sentence on each test and special project paper. At the end of the test, students write sentences that explain their effort and the amount of study time given to the assignment. Below are actual Honor Sentences that have shown up on my students' papers. These illustrate the depth of learning about integrity and accountability.

This is my own work. I studied for twenty minutes each night for three nights.

I passed this test with an A+ because I studied really long and hard. I went the extra mile!

I put things off this week and studied only fifteen minutes. I know I failed the test—but at least it is my own work. I did not cheat.

I didn't study at all for this test. I promise to try harder next time.

I studied my brains out, and I feel really good on this one!

I studied two hours, and my mom helped. I think I did really well!

This is not my own work. I'm sorry, can I talk to you about it?

I took this test seriously. I gave it a lot of study time. I'm sure I got an A!

I studied each night this week. It was worth it!

One thing I like about using this practice is that it develops accountability. The students know that they will have to disclose the amount of study time devoted to their assignments. There is no escaping it. They also know that there will be consequences when they choose not to study and rewards when they do. A nice thing about this practice is that it becomes second nature for students. They develop the habit of writing their sentence without being reminded. One time that I was absent from school, I forgot to tell my substitute about it in my lesson plans. She left me a note and commented on how the students reminded her—and each other—about the Honor Sentence. She thought it was a good idea.

Perhaps what I like best about this activity is that students eventually come to understand that their grades are most often earned in direct proportion to the amount of time and effort put forth in study. Writing this sentence takes only a moment, but goes a long way in helping students to develop a work ethic that translates into academic achievement!

63 From Work Ethic to Life Ethic

Helping your students to develop a positive work ethic just may be one of the most important things you can do! A child's work ethic begins in his first year of schooling and continues on throughout life. Each decision a child makes either adds to that positive work ethic or detracts from it.

> "Learning about good character helps you try harder than ever to reach your goal of earning a spot on the A Honor Roll. Then you feel good about yourself that you can achieve excellence!"
>
> —Samara, age 11

I believe that it is a teacher's calling to help children learn to make more deposits in their work ethic account and fewer withdrawals. It is that calling to personal excellence that will translate into academic success. And of course, both personal and academic excellence will translate into a work ethic that transcends the school experience. I believe that a child's work ethic in school will become his life ethic. So from school climate to curriculum to the world of work, a positive work ethic is a grand goal for all of us.

64 Teacher Modeling

There is no doubt about it, kids watch our every move. From the way we dress, to the way we talk, to the way we treat others, kids pay attention! They watch for discrepancies in our message and our modeling. They don't miss a trick. Therefore, we must know and understand that *the walk* is more powerful than *the talk*.

Students don't just watch our every move in the classroom. They watch how we treat and interact with the other teachers on the staff. They watch our day-to-day words and actions, our facial expressions and our body language. They look to see if we are demonstrating the traits of good character that we espouse.

They also watch to see if we take our own education seriously. After all, if we don't, why should they? It makes an important impression when they hear on the morning announcements that the graduate class will meet each Tuesday or that the staff development session this month will be on reading strategies. They are interested in the books we read and the classes we take. They need to know that learning is a lifelong process, and that the hard work involved in the pursuit of furthering our education is worthwhile.

Often I will bring a book to school that I am reading and just lay it on my desk. It is a great conversation starter at break time or before and after school. Kids will respect your teachings more if they know that there is something of substance behind all that you do. In fact, I always remind them of a comment that Michelangelo made shortly before his death: *I am still learning!*

65 Our Decisions Define Us!

In fact, these very words are written on the wall. This is such an important teaching message for me and my students that this sentence runs along the top of one of my classroom walls. In large, colorful letters, the message is spelled out in a big way. I don't believe that there is a day that I haven't referred to it in some way.

Our decisions to be kind or cruel, sympathetic or unfeeling, respectful or disrespectful will help to determine the kind of person we become. Our decisions to do our homework or not, to listen in class or not, to try our best or not, will help to determine what kind of student we become. Each decision we make—large or small—will add or detract from our total being. So for building an academic climate in your classroom and school, remind your students of this powerful and life-changing lesson: *Our decisions define us!*

66 Responsible Students

Every school in our district must have some kind of written plan for promoting student behavior and responsibility. The plan must address discipline as well as academics. It's a good safeguard for assuring that student behavior will not distract from the academic learning opportunities in the school.

Each year, the plan is revised along with the School Improvement Plan. Our staff sits down and discusses the school year. We bring up all of the problems as well as all of the successes. We make suggestions on how we can make next year's plan better for students to follow and for parents to understand. Something that has helped strengthen our Responsible Students Plan in recent years has been the weaving of character education into that plan. Teaching character gives the plan substance, as well as strength.

The expectations are posted in every room of the school, and a list of rules is given to each student to take home to their parents. They are reprinted for you here so you can see exactly what I am referring to. As you read through the list, take time to notice how character is woven into the plan.

The plan is built with student rewards and consequences. Consistency, of course, is the key to the plan's success. Remember that kids will try you at every turn. It's sad to say, but often parents will do the same. They will ask you to make an exception, just this once. If the entire staff is consistent and fair, the plan works wonderfully well. Remember, you are in the driver's seat on this one.

Weimer C.A.R.E.S.
RESPECT AND RESPONSIBILITIES

Red...**respect!**
- Listen
- Show respect
- Use good manners
- Work cooperatively
- Follow classroom rules
- Follow school rules

Blue...**responsibility!**
- Come prepared for class
- Work independently
- Complete assignments
- Turn in homework
- Return permission slips promptly
- Return office communications
- Return library books
- Organize materials and workspace
- Organize self and belongings

Green...**quiet times!**
- In school hallways
- In line
- During fire drills
- During shelter-in-place
- During intercom announcements
- When a visitor enters the room
- During a test
- During silent reading

Purple...**cafeteria!**
- Get supplies on your way through the line
- Use a soft and respectful voice
- Show proper table manners
- Stay in your seat at all times
- Be respectful of others at your table
- Clean up...pick up!

Guidelines...
for rewards and consequences!
- 3 violations of the same color in one month = counseling referral slip
- 6 violations in one month = parent notification slip
- 9 monthly violations allowed per student
- 10 monthly violations = no C.A.R.E.S. reward plus a discipline slip
- 15 monthly violations = suspension or parent spending the day with student

Discipline Slips...
given for these behaviors!
- Disrespectful behavior
- Cafeteria problem
- Disruptive conduct
- Inappropriate language
- Failure to obey authority
- Inappropriate dress
- Failure to work to full potential

67 Interjections!

This strategy got its start in one of my math classes. We were working on a difficult math skill and the students were really struggling. I could tell that they were on the verge of giving up. To keep them from becoming discouraged, I stopped the math lesson and interjected an inspirational story about Dr. Norman Vincent Peale. It seems that Dr. Peale encountered numerous rejections from publishers for his book, *The Power of Positive Thinking*. With the last rejection, he came home and put the complete manuscript into the wastebasket. "I quit!" he announced to his wife Ruth. "I'm not going to try for publication anymore," he told her.

Ruth was a loyal wife. She consoled and encouraged Norman. She asked him to try again. She even offered to help. "I forbid you to take this manuscript out of the wastebasket, Ruth," he reprimanded. "It's over. I'm giving up."

The next day, Ruth put on her coat and hat. Honoring her husband's feelings on the matter, she went to his office and picked up the wastebasket. She left with that wastebasket and a list of publishers' addresses. Upon entering the office of the first publisher, she simply placed the wastebasket on his desk. "My husband forbid me to take his manuscript out of the wastebasket, but he didn't mention anything about you doing it." She smiled.

After taking a good look at the manuscript, the publisher offered Dr. Peale his first book contract. The rest is history!

When I told my students how many millions of books Dr. Peale has sold all over the world, they were impressed. They also quickly came to the conclusion that if his wife had given up on him, that Dr. Peale wouldn't have ever known the success that was only one step away.

This interjected story did more than motivate the kids to keep trying, it inspired them to look for their talents and abilities and to plan for their futures. So, when you see that your students need a little motivation and inspiration, use interjections! The determination that they interject can make a big academic difference in the life of your kids!

68 Look for the Lesson

No matter what the subject matter, no matter what the lesson of the day—students will come to learn more about the character message when it is woven into all that you do. Calling your students' attention to the *lesson within the lesson* is a powerful way to show that life's greatest lessons can be found within our studies at school. In fact, if we learn to pay attention, they can be found just about anywhere!

Examples of lessons from different areas of the curriculum are illustrated below.

LESSON	THE CHARACTER LESSON WITHIN
Martin Luther King, Jr.	Respect, fairness, citizenship
The Making of the American Flag	Citizenship
George Washington, Abe Lincoln	Honesty, bravery
Louis Slotkin	Accountability, integrity, respect
The Tortoise and the Hare	Perseverance
The Schooling of Afghanistan Children	Fairness, respect
Ruby Bridges	Respect, fairness, bravery, citizenship
Math: coins, money	Honesty
Aristotle	Virtue, character, work ethic
World Cultures and Religions	Respect
Thomas Edison and Electricity	Perseverance
Mother Teresa	Respect, caring, compassion, service
Aesop's Fables	Every character trait is represented

69 Peer Tutoring

When high school students from Service Learning Class come to help at your school, let them get involved in a peer-tutoring program. High school students can be a wonderful asset in helping your elementary kids practice and master basic skills. Extra help and practice with math, spelling, and reading skills, or even difficult science concepts, can go a long way in helping younger students meet with success. Sometimes just the companionship and closeness of an older student reading a story to a younger child or listening to the younger child read is motivation for extra effort in skill development. And the older student also benefits! High school students learn to be positive role models for younger kids and learn to give back to the communities of which they are a part. The teamwork and camaraderie built will help both the elementary school and high school grow strong.

> Sometimes, just the companionship and closeness of an older student reading a story to a younger child or listening to the younger child read is motivation for extra effort in skill development.

70 Monthly Goal-Setting Sessions

Remember the research from Chapter One about the power of setting goals and writing them down? I'll review: 87% of people do not have goals, 10% have goals, and 3% commit their goals in writing. Those who write down their goals achieve 50-100 times *more* than those who simply think about and talk about their goals. We want our students to become members of *The 3% Club*! And remember, with 90-95% of what we do each day attributed to habit, we want for our kids to develop *good* habits. Setting goals and working towards them is one way to get there!

In my monthly goal setting sessions with students, I help them work on several kinds of goals: academic goals, personal goals, and social goals. I want for them to become well-rounded people. Academic goals will help them with their studies and grades, personal goals will help them to become all that they can be, and social goals will help them in their interactions with others. Each month, we choose a new goal in each area to work on. We write down the goals and commit them to memory.

During the month, we pull out our goal lists and see how we are doing. We chart our progress, we make adjustments. We resolve to work harder. The first month of school, we post our goals in the classroom near the door. That makes it a little easier for students to see them on a daily basis. It helps them stay focused. Whether your students keep their goal lists in their notebooks, lockers, and backpacks or on display in the classroom is not important. What is important is that they take the time to set goals, write them down and keep check on their progress. That's what *growing in goodness* is all about!

Over the years while teaching the Character Class for my K-6 students, I have kept copies of their goal lists. I have selected a sample to include in this book. Perhaps these will help you to see what kinds of thing students have chosen to work on over the course of the school year.

Student Academic Goals

- To stay on task
- To be a better listener
- To do my homework
- To be a better reader
- To improve my handwriting
- To be responsible for my assignments
- To have a better report card
- To get straight A's
- To make the Honor Roll
- To get in a good college
- To get a job that I like
- To follow directions
- To learn math facts
- To follow school rules
- To try my best

Student Social Goals

- To be nice to my sister
- To change my attitude
- To make new friends
- To be a better teammate in basketball
- To follow the Golden Rule
- To be respectful with my parents
- To tell the truth all the time
- To control my temper
- To listen when my friends are talking
- To be helpful
- To take turns
- To share with others
- To be kind to everyone

Student Personal Goals

- To learn to do a handspring
- To complete a 500-piece puzzle
- To play basketball for UNC
- To be a cartoonist
- To learn to play an instrument
- To learn sign language
- To dive off of the high dive
- To eat healthy
- To be more lovable
- To do more good deeds
- To watch less television
- To start saving money
- To spend more time with my family
- To have a good time without being bad

Remember that there are two kinds of goals: long-term goals and short-term goals. Kids need to learn to set both kinds. And remember to teach students to be *specific* when setting their goals. The more specific students are in setting goals, the better chance they will have of reaching them. In the list above, one student did that quite well. He not only wants to go to college and play basketball; he has chosen the school, the University of North Carolina.

71 Report Card Goal-Setting Sessions

Students need to see that their schoolwork and goals are connected. This practice will help students to focus on their studies and to work towards academic success. On the day that students will be receiving their report cards, I hand out the Goal Setting Session worksheets. Each student writes his name and the date on the top of the sheet.

The first section of the worksheet is for predicting what grades the students think they *earned* for this grading period. Notice that I am careful to use the word *earned*, rather than the word *got*. The language here is quite important. I want my students to understand that I don't *give* grades. I simply record the grades that they *earn*. The second section of the worksheet is for recording the grades that students earned during the previous grading period. The reason for this section is so that a comparison can be made.

Then I pass out the student report cards. They open them up and look them over. They then move on to the third section of the worksheet. It is in this spot that they record their newly earned grades. Question number four is simple: Did your grades go up or down? Then comes the part where students have to dig deeply for answers: Give the *reasons* for any changes in your grades.

Students now have to face the music. There is no room for excuses. We are developing accountability for our decisions of the last nine weeks. As a teacher, it is interesting to observe. Students become excited when they see that their grades have improved, and they come to understand that extra study time and effort were the reasons for the change. It is sad to see those who have not measured up. But there is hope! Students are enlightened when they begin admitting that poor study habits, laziness, and irresponsibility have been contributing factors to their failures. I remind them that it is never too late to change.

The logical next step is planning for the future. We take a few minutes to think about our habits—really think! We develop goals for the coming grading period. These goals will be helpful in improving our work ethic and our grades. We set to work. All in all, this is about a twenty-minute activity. Yes, it does take time out of our instructional day. But the way I see it, this is part of the most important instruction of all. Students come to see the direct correlation between work ethic and academic success. Plus you get the added incentive of knowing that it is never too late to wipe the slate clean and change your ways. I have seen students go from D's to B's and stay there!

Goal-Setting Session
End of the Nine-Week Grading Period

Name_____ Date _____

1. Predict what grades you think you *earned* this grading period:

   Reading _____   Social Studies _____
   English _____   Science _____
   Spelling _____   Health _____
   Math _____   Citizenship _____

2. Record what grades you *earned* last nine weeks in these subjects:

   Reading _____   Social Studies _____
   English _____   Science _____
   Spelling _____   Health _____
   Math _____   Citizenship _____

3. Write down the new grades you *earned* for this grading period:

   Reading _____   Social Studies _____
   English _____   Science _____
   Spelling _____   Health _____
   Math _____   Citizenship _____

4. Did your grades go up or down?

   _____

5. Give the *reasons* for the changes in your grades:

   _____
   _____
   _____

6. Write down five goals for improving your work ethic and grades:

   _____
   _____
   _____
   _____
   _____

Join the 3% club!

72 Character Journals

I have been doing Character Journals for years, and they are my very favorite character-building practice of all. Considering the amount of time they take, and the difference they make, you've just *got* to try them!

It's easy. We use those black-and-white composition books, but any kind of a notebook will do. Each morning I have a character quote on the chalkboard when students arrive. I always write down the same one that I put on the morning announcements for the day. Writing down the quote of the day simply becomes part of the morning routine: go to your locker, get your books and supplies for the day, graph in for attendance and lunch, put your homework in the basket, and write in your Character Journal. It's as simple as that. Writing down the quote takes all of one minute. And all of this happens before the tardy bell even rings.

But don't stop there. Use that quote throughout the day. Repeat it during the transition times of the day: when lining up to go to gym class, lunch, or the library or when packing backpacks at the end of the day. As Aristotle taught us, repetition is the mother of skill.

Another great idea is to have the older kids write a *reflection paragraph* about the quote on days when there is time. Students can write about what the quote means and how they might put the wisdom to work in their own life. This extension activity takes a few minutes more, but is worth the time and effort that it takes. Since students are writing, this activity can be woven in with the language arts lesson of the day.

Character quotes are just one of the things that students put in their journals. Whenever I find a good story that can be typed up on one page, I run copies for my class. The students staple them in and write a paragraph of reflection about the story. Copies of good editorial cartoons and stories from the newspaper are also good journal entries. I have also been known to include the heroes column from *The Reader's Digest* and other uplifting stories. Articles showcasing good character from your local newspaper are also good to copy and pass out to students.

By the end of the year, I usually have about 180 good character quotes, ten good stories, twelve teaching cartoons, nine hero stories, and dozens of pages of written reflections. When students leave at the end of the school year, they have a wonderful book of wisdom to take with them. Parents and students both cherish that collection. It is my favorite thing to send with them as they walk off into their futures!

73 Write On!

Some kids have taken their Character Journals a step further by using them to carry the character message to others. You will smile with pride after reading about Carol and Cody. After reading of their troubles earlier in this book, you will see how their Character Journals changed the lives of those they touched.

One of my troubled sixth-grade students was expelled from school and spent the remainder of the school year in an alternative school. Carol took her Character

Journal with her to her new school. Each month I would mail Carol new quotes to write in her journal. Anything that we were doing at school made its way to Carol in the mail. An administrator from her new school called me about a month after Carol had enrolled. She was impressed by Carol's knowledge of the quotes and character wisdom in that journal. She said that Carol had literally committed the entire journal of quotes to memory! She asked for permission to use Character Journals with the students in that alternative school. I was thrilled! She also shared with me the plans to videotape Carol teaching other students about good character from the wisdom in her journal. The administrators in the alternative school believed that Character Journals held the power to help all of their troubled students.

Although troubled by the home life that she had endured for her entire childhood, Carol had that moral rope of character instruction to hang on to. She hung on tightly to that rope and journal! I honestly think that was all that Carol had in her sad life to help her try to overcome her upbringing and her environment. Not a day goes by in the classroom that I don't think of Carol when I am writing that quote on the chalkboard. I know that this is a practice I will keep for as long as I teach!

Another touching result of Character Journals comes from my former kindergarten student, Cody. He is the student who changed my life with the story of his dad who was in prison. Cody came to see me one day about three years ago. It seems that Cody had been sending character quotes to his dad in prison. He had taught his dad how to write them down and study them in an attempt to straighten out his life. That simple act had given Cody's dad the motivation to take courses to get his high school equivalency diploma. So, when Cody's dad is released on parole in several years, he will walk out of prison a smarter and better man. He will have his high school degree and a course in character under his belt. I told you earlier, and I still believe it, sometimes *kids* are the very best teachers of all. I think that Carol and Cody prove the point!

So many days we go into our classroom with ideas on what we are going to teach children. Try going in to your classroom and being open to the idea of what you ar able to learn... from them!

74 Success Library

Reading is so important! Because I believe that children become better readers by actually reading, I keep lots of books on hand in the classroom. I bring books from home and I write grants to buy even more. What kind of books do I keep in the collection? Success books!

Books that I call *success books* are ones that build character. These are books that help you, guide you, and point you in the direction of achieving personal, academic, and professional success. They are the books that are found in the self-help and psychology sections of bookstores. They are also the little life-lesson books found in gift shops. Books on confidence, character, and courage. Books on determination and desire. Books that include the wisdom of the generations. Books that inspire and motivate you to be the best person that you can be. In my opinion, we don't read enough of them!

Start building a collection for your class. For a first step, I just got a big basket and filled it with books from home. I was amazed at how the kids enjoyed reading them. And because they were my personal books, the students were extra careful and respectful of them. They grabbed a book for some *success reading* whenever there was a free moment, whenever they had finished their class work and even during recess on a rainy day. Reading positive and uplifting books supports students on their journey to goodness!

Here are a few titles to help get you started.

The Book of Virtues	William Bennett
The Children's Book of Virtues	William Bennett
The Children's Book of Heroes	William Bennett
The Children's Book of America	William Bennett
Our Country's Founders	William Bennett
The Moral Compass	William Bennett
Life's Greatest Lessons	Hal Urban
Chicken Soup for the Children's Soul	Jack Canfield /Mark Victor Hansen
Life's Little Instruction Book	H. Jackson Brown, Jr.
Live and Learn and Pass It On	H. Jackson Brown, Jr.
Notes from a Friend	Anthony Robbins
100 Days of Growing Rich	Napoleon Hill
Kid's Little Instruction Book	Jim and Steve Dodson
Zig Ziglar's Little Instruction Book	Zig Ziglar
A Call to Character	Greer/Kohl
Winning Words of Champions	Larry Bielat
A Return to Virtue	Bell/Campbell
The 7 Habits of Highly Effective Teens	Sean Covey
Speaking of Character	Michael Mitchell and Bill Wotring
The Portable Pep Talk	Alexander Lockhart
Positive Charges	Alexander Lockhart

75 Read Aloud!

All children love to be read to. When I left kindergarten and moved to sixth grade, I took with me the habit of reading to my students. I was surprised at how much the older kids enjoyed it. The practice models good oral reading skills and gets students excited about books and stories. It also forms a bond between you and your students. How do you weave the character message into your stories? Easy! Just select stories from good literature that have moral lessons, noble characters, and honest plots. And a little discussion at the end of the story is always a grand idea!

76 Aesop's Fables

I was raised on Aesop. My great-grandmother, Maw Great, told me his fables while I was growing up. There was always a lesson to be learned.

Aesop was a Phrygian slave who lived around the sixth century B.C. Just like Uncle Remus, Aesop told his best stories about birds and beasts. His animal stories are built on the firm foundations of common sense and integrity that are very much a part of the human element. These fables have helped generations of children have a moral rope to hang on to when contemplating their decisions and actions.

More than two thousand years later, Aesop's stories are still powerful in transmitting to children the value of good decisions in life. School year after school year, it is always the same. I share the timeless wisdom by reading and discussing the stories of Aesop. Who can forget the tortoise and the hare? Slow and steady wins the race! What a great story for teaching the character traits of perseverance and determination. We read them all year long. You could, too. A list follows to help motivate you to read some of Aesop's best!

- The Fox and the Grapes   *Never give up!*
- The Ants and the Grasshopper   *Work before play!*
- The Tortoise and the Hare   *Slow and steady wins the race!*
- The Mouse at the Seashore   *Hard work pays off!*
- The Crow and the Pitcher   *Little by little does the trick!*
- The Lion and the Mouse   *Small friends can be great friends!*
- The Cat and the Mouse   *To have a friend...be a friend!*

A nice way to extend your study of Aesop is to do puppet shows with his stories. I wrote a classroom mini-grant and received five hundred dollars to supplement my Aesop Unit. That bought just about every kind of animal puppet available! My students enjoy giving the puppet shows to our entire school community. Young and old alike enjoy the timeless wisdom of Aesop's fables. They are a fun and easy way to share the character message with just about anyone.

77 Just Play!

Literature provides lots of stories, poems, and ideas that can be woven with the character message. Elementary kids love plays. Choral readings, short plays, and puppet shows are all wonderful and creative ways to explore the world of literature and character at the same time. These can be buddy-projects between older and younger students in the school, or they can be done within your own classroom. Older elementary students can even write their own stories and present them to other classes in the school. Students will enjoy doing what comes naturally for them while working on the projects...playing!

78 Heroes in Character

Heroes are role models for all kids. But heroes and celebrities are not the same. Kids need to know the difference. Reading, Social Studies, Literature and History classes are all great places to drive home the fact. When studying famous people, weave the character thread into the fabric of your class discussions. We keep a Heroes Chart on our classroom wall and in our Character Journals to record the names and deeds of those who measure up. Here are some of our favorites.

J.C. Penney	Great work ethic, treated customers and employees with respect, called his stores Golden Rule Stores
Mother Teresa	Showed caring and compassion
Louis Slotkin	Showed caring, took responsibility for his actions
Martin Luther King, Jr.	Showed respect, fairness, citizenship
Ben and Jerry	Show responsibility in taking care of the environment by giving farmers their empty ice cream buckets
Frank Daily	Showed caring by giving his shoes to a lady who had none
New York firefighters	Showed bravery and caring by rescuing victims of the World Trade Center
American citizens	Showed caring and citizenship by giving money and time
George W. Bush	Showed bravery and citizenship by taking a stand against terrorism

Parents have heroes, too. One of the homework assignments I give each school year is for students and their parents to discuss the difference between celebrities and heroes. Both are then to make a list of three personal heroes and send the list back to class. This activity promotes meaningful dialogue between children and their parents. It also gets both thinking about what kind of behavior they respect, admire, and look up to. Here are a few samples of parent heroes from over the years. Take a look!

John Wayne	Made decent movies
Princess Diana	Showed compassion and caring, and helped others
Ronald Reagan	Brought peace by stopping the war
Mickey Mantle	Played great baseball and always tried his best
Mary Kay Ash	Built her cosmetic business on the Golden Rule
Mother Teresa	Lived out her lifetime commitment to care for the poor
Jerry West	Practiced a good work ethic to achieve athletic greatness
Jeff Gordon	Always shows good sportsmanship
Eleanor Roosevelt	Showed strength and determination

79 Character in the Workplace

When I started teaching sixth grade, I ran across a Scholastic book in our reading series called *From Rags To Riches*. It is filled with wonderful stories of American businesses that were started from scratch and went on to become successful. I saw this book as an opportunity to teach about the importance of work ethic while teaching reading.

I wrote a nine-week unit that I called *Character and Ethics in the American Workplace*. We read, discussed, and studied the stories of people and businesses that lived and worked by the Golden Rule. Ben and Jerry, J.C. Penney, Marriott Hotels, Hewlett Packard, Hershey's, Dow Jones and *The Wall Street Journal*, Apple Computers, Cisco Systems and MindSpring were just some of the businesses we studied. For each business we created semantic maps about their work ethic, and at the end of the nine weeks students were beginning to see the connection between character and success. It was a joy to see!

During this study unit, we used many instructional strategies to promote higher level thinking skills. We wove the character message into each strategy: class discussions, semantic maps, graphs, K-W-L charts, brainstorming charts, and Venn diagrams. We used Think-Ink-Speak and Think-Pair-Share. We wrote essays and reports. We had business representatives visit and talk with our class. We visited a business in our area. We did it all! And I am happy to say that the character message weaves well into each instructional strategy and activity. It's a natural thread in the fabric of the classroom!

80 Spelling for Character

In my sixth-grade spelling text there are ten words for the week, with suggestions for ten more. The list is made up with words that are characteristic of the certain skill being taught. A great way to weave character into your spelling curriculum is to select character words to fill in the list to make twenty words. I can always find a few words in the auxiliary list that I can use to make the character connection. Words like *environment* and *litter* can be tied to the trait of good citizenship. Words like *honesty* and *integrity* are obvious shoo-ins.

The character connection can be built with words from every level of the elementary school curriculum. Lower level words like *nice, kind, hope,* and *try* all fit well when spelling for character. I even give a character word or two as bonus words for the week. Students will study those in an effort to earn bonus points on their spelling grade. But as you can guess, they learn and earn much more than points in this assignment.

enviro**n**ment

hon**n**esty

81 The Academic Connection

If the character message weaves so easily into the fabric of reading, writing, social studies, history, spelling, and literature, how can we continue the weaving into all aspects of the elementary school curriculum? Just creating awareness is an important first step. Then you will naturally come to look for ways to do the weaving. You will find small, but important, ways to connect the subject matter with the character message. Honesty at test-taking time, integrity during mathematics calculations, and respectful listening during class discussions are only a few. Just pointing out these small lessons will add up in big ways to transform your classroom. So start out small and grow as the year progresses. The progress you see with your students will propel you onward. Pretty soon, you will become an expert at seeing the connection. You will see opportunities to weave the character message into *all* that you do!

> You will find small, but important, ways to connect the subject matter with the character message.

82 Weekly Communication Folder

Communicating with the home is one of the most important aspects of teaching. We all know that a home and school that work together sends a powerful message about the importance of an education. It is vital to send a message to the home about the importance of character, as well.

Each week, I am careful to get all of my students' papers and tests graded. By Monday we are ready to share the previous week's work with the parents. We take the time on Monday to pass out the week's papers. The kids love doing this! It gets them involved in organizing their work and reporting it to their parents. This takes about ten to fifteen minutes of class time, but it is well worth the effort.

Each child has a Weekly Communication Folder. As the week's papers are passed out, each student puts his papers in the folder—in any order he wishes. It is cute to see how they choose to arrange them! Many decide to put the best-graded papers first, and hide trouble spots among the ones in the back. Some will cleverly choose to put the worst first to get it over with, and use the great grades as the icing on the cake!

Along with their weekly papers go their computer reports for the week, any correspondence from any of the other specialty teachers in the building, and any office communication that needs to go home. But in the most prominent place in the folder, right in front, is the Weekly Communication Sheet.

This is the summary sheet, the tell-all device that I use to let parents know the whole story! It is simple to design, simple to run off and simple to do. Now I admit that it does take about thirty minutes out of each weekend for me to fill them out for my twenty-eight students and to run copies for my files. But it may be about the best-spent thirty minutes of the week!

There are three possible marks given: a star means *excellent*, a plus sign means *satisfactory*, and a minus sign indicates that *improvement is needed*. It's as simple as that. What are the areas that I evaluate? Manners, respect, listening, effort, work ethic, and behavior. I also leave a place for the number of rule violations and missing assignments. Even though the students are not allowed to make up unexcused missing work, the missing assignments are there in black and white. It sure goes a long way towards explaining why grades might be low at report card time!

And don't forget the commendations! Always take a minute to jot down something to celebrate. Students need feedback; they need to know that you notice and appreciate their hard work. And they need affirmation and praise for a job well done. One sincere comment in this section helps to motivate a student to continue working diligently.

Once the sheet is filled out and copied, it goes in the front of the folder. Parents know to look for it, and students have the choice about what goes on that sheet. If they work hard and behave well, the sheet looks great and they are proud to take it home. If they have made bad choices and let their responsibilities slip, they have no one to blame for the negative feel of the communication sheet.

The last part of this strategy is the parent's responsibility. Stapled to the inside cover of the folder is the Parent Signature Sheet. It has a place for a parent signature for each week of the school year. When the parent signs, he takes responsibility for seeing, discussing, and knowing about his child's progress in school.

I keep a copy of each child's Weekly Communication Sheet in his folder. At the end of the year, there is a clear record of growth for each child. This comes in handy at conference time. Parents cannot say that they *didn't know* there were academic or behavior concerns. They have been updated each and every week. Molehills do not become mountains when the communication between school and home is ongoing and consistent throughout the school year!

Parent Signature Sheet

Week	Week
1 _____	18 _____
2 _____	19 _____
3 _____	20 _____
4 _____	21 _____
5 _____	22 _____
6 _____	23 _____
7 _____	24 _____
8 _____	25 _____
9 _____	26 _____
10 _____	27 _____
11 _____	28 _____
12 _____	29 _____
13 _____	30 _____
14 _____	31 _____
15 _____	32 _____
16 _____	33 _____
17 _____	34 _____

Weekly Communication Sheet

Student Name _____

Date _____

Shows manners and respect   _____
Follows rules and procedures   _____
Listens to teacher and instruction _____
Work ethic/best effort   _____
Number of rule violations   _____
Number of missing assignments   _____

KEY
* Excellent
+ Acceptable
- Needs Improvement

83 The Homework Basket

The Homework Basket doesn't seem like it could be a curriculum-building strategy, does it? But there is more to this story than meets the eye! I have always found it to be a good way to help your students develop a good work ethic. Here's how. Simply tell your students what it means to put an assignment into this basket. Turning in an assignment means that the student is telling his teacher this: *Ms. Brown, I am finished with my homework. I have given this assignment my best effort. I have really worked hard. My paper is complete, neatly written, and well thought out. I am proud of my work, and I am now ready for you to read it!*

After putting this new slant on things, I think that you will notice students taking that basket a little more seriously. Rather than it being a place to put assignments that they finish in a hurry, your students will come to respect what that basket really stands for. I have seen students walk up, place their paper in the basket, pause in thought, and then pull it right back out again. They have obviously reflected on the assignment at hand and realized that they could have done better. Revising our work in this way helps students go beyond *mediocrity* to the *excellence* we have been talking about!

84 Homework in Character

Thursday is character homework night. I intentionally give students an assignment that will help them on their journey to becoming better people. It isn't a big assignment, just one they can do in fifteen to twenty minutes. The difference it has made has been monumental. Why? Because we squeeze in thirty-five of these assignments during the course of a school year. Sometimes I send home a copy of a thoughtful story or article that addresses the topic of good character. The students are told to read the selection and to write down the main ideas and a few supporting points from the story. They are to be ready to take part in a follow-up class discussion the next day. I also have them share the story with their parents. This is an important part of the homework assignment. It is the way that I let students take home the character message. They carry it home in their backpacks!

Sometimes the assignment is simple: Look up the word *respect* in your dictionary. Of course, this is an assignment in spelling and study skills—as well as an assignment in character. Discuss with your parents several ways of showing respect. Write down your family's five favorite ideas and bring them to school and share in the class discussion.

Responses from even the youngest students show their growing insight into character development.

- knocking before entering
- holding the door for people
- saying *sir* and *ma'am*
- saying *thank you*
- being polite
- listening when others talk to you
- shaking hands
- answering the phone in a polite way
- picking up after yourself
- being grateful
- following The Golden Rule

Sometimes the homework assignment is to look for *Character in the News*. Students are to peruse newspapers and magazines for a story or article that could make for an interesting discussion on character. Sample articles have included: John Glenn's trip into space (work ethic, determination, pursuit of your dreams), the Columbine shooting (respect and caring for others, doing the right thing), a story about girls in Afghanistan being denied the opportunity to go to school (fairness, respect), and an article on Mary Kay Cosmetics (the company ehtic is based on the Golden Rule). The discussions that start at home and continue at school are very effective in making the language of character clear and consistent. By using the newspaper and magazines, it is easy to find current event situations to discuss. These character assignments let parents know what you stand for and encourage them to further their child's character development at home! (For more ideas and actual assignments for every week of the school year, please see the *Character Messages* section near the end of this book.)

85 The Book of Virtues

If you have a teacher's desk, some paper and an empty three-ring binder, you're all set for this one. As I said earlier in the book, I have a desk but I hardly ever sit there during the school day. But that is where I keep our class *Book of Virtues*. I got this idea a few years ago after William Bennett's book came out. I thought of all of the wonderful character traits that were illustrated in that book. So I thought that it might be nice to illustrate a few of our own. I made up a form for the entry and ran lots of copies. I put them in a basket near my desk. Inside the three-ring binder, I put in nine dividers—each marked with a character trait: honesty, trustworthiness, caring, respect, work ethic, fairness, perseverance, responsibility, and citizenship. Whenever a student finished his work early or had extra time, he could go and sit at my desk and work on an entry. He would put his name and the date at the top of the paper. He would then fill in the name of the character trait for the entry. Then the student could draw a picture to illustrate the trait. Below the illustration, he would then write a few words about the trait of good character.

The younger elementary students do a wonderful job with this activity. Six-year-old Megan proved the point. About mid-morning of this special day, Megan wrote her very first sentences of the school year. Megan had figured out that if she copied the names of her classmates from their crayon boxes, that she could  write as many new sentences as there were students in the class. She set to work. In her journal that morning, Megan wrote the following sentences: *I like Will. I like Brooke. I like Chris. I like Jeff....* Megan was so excited that she filled the front and back of the page with sentences. It was fun to watch her get the hang of writing!

Later that morning, Megan put her pencil behind her ear and went into the bathroom. She was in there for quite a while. She finally came out and joined us for a story. The next student stepped inside and closed the door. He came right back out and interrupted with an announcement, "Someone has written all over the bathroom wall! They wrote all kinds of sentences: I like Will. I like Brooke. I like Chris. They wrote about everybody!" Now I *had* to ask the question. But no one owned up to the writing. Since we were getting ready to have story time, I simply grabbed the book on Pinocchio and began reading. A few minutes later, Megan jumped up to interrupt the story and made her confession, "I did it, I did it! I wrote on the bathroom wall."

"Megan, I am very proud of you for telling the truth. I'm sure you know that it is disrespectful to write on the wall. I hope that you will not do it again. Now please go in there and try to erase your sentences." When Megan came out of the restroom, she went right to my desk and started writing in the *Book of Virtues*. When she finished her entry, she asked if she could read it to the class. Megan stood before her classmates and read her sentence: *I told the truth*. Another classmate, recalling the writing process that we use in our room, made an editing suggestion, "Megan, you had better revise that sentence to read: I *finally* told the truth!"

I couldn't help but smile.

Over the course of the school year, many entries made their way into that notebook. The students loved making the book and would take it from my desk just to browse through it and read. The very young students will need help with their sentences. They will need help sounding out and spelling the words. Spelling the names of the character traits *is* very difficult for them. But with a list posted in the front of the book, even kindergarten students can sound out and figure out the words and then copy them.

The students get their ideas from every experience you provide during the course of the year. Stories, lessons, discussions, and real-life experiences have all provided inspiration. I have included a few of the entries so you can get a feel for the student ideas that went into our notebook.

<table>
<tr><td>Perseverance</td><td>Slow and steady wins the race.</td></tr>
<tr><td>Work Ethic</td><td>I want to be able to slam dunk a basketball.</td></tr>
<tr><td>Responsibility</td><td>I help take care of my little sister.</td></tr>
<tr><td>Caring</td><td>Me and my reading buddy are friends.</td></tr>
<tr><td>Citizenship</td><td>I pick up litter on the playground.</td></tr>
<tr><td>Fairness</td><td>Rosa Parks wanted to be treated with respect.</td></tr>
<tr><td>Kindness</td><td>I am nice to my mom.</td></tr>
<tr><td>Responsibility</td><td>Louis Slotkin took responsibility for his mistake.</td></tr>
<tr><td>Honesty</td><td>George Washington admitted cutting down the tree.</td></tr>
<tr><td>Honesty</td><td>I finally told the truth!</td></tr>
</table>

> "Even when it's tough, dig down inside yourself and find the strength to do the right thing. Don't do what's easy... do what's right!"
>
> —Maw Great

86 Chain of Responsibility

Teachers are always looking for a way to help their students learn responsibility skills. There is a definite academic connection! Elementary students need constant reinforcement of this important life lesson. One way to teach the skill is to work with students on making a chain of responsibility. You can do the chain in one day and add to it as the year progresses. Or you can start slowly and develop the strategy over a period of time. Or you can start during a teachable moment and go from there. The possibilities are endless!

Here's how it works. Have some paper cut and ready to go. I use strips of colored paper that are about six inches long by one inch wide, roughly the size you use when making paper chains at Christmas. Each student puts his name on the first link. On the second link, you write the behavior, followed by its consequence on the third link. Each consequence will be followed by a new behavior and then, of course, a new consequence. Students will begin to see how good decisions create a chain of positive events, while poor decisions lead to a chain of negative consequences.

I always do a class chain as an example before letting students try this on their own. Here is the first one I made up to show them. Perhaps it will help give you ideas for a starting place.

Link #1	I decided to do my homework.
Link #2	I got a good grade on it.
Link #3	It helped me learn the material.
Link #4	I did well on my weekly test.
Link #5	My parents were proud of my test grade.
Link #6	It made me want to do better in school.
Link #7	I started doing my homework each night.
Link #8	I began to study more for tests.
Link #9	At report card time, I made the Honor Roll.
Link #10	My parents were excited...and so was I!
Link #11	I got to go on the Honor Roll Field Trip!
Link #12	It felt good to see my name in the school newspaper for something good!

Once your students write down and link together the positive or negative events and the ensuing consequences, they will be one step closer to understanding the powerful connection between actions and consequences. This is one chain of events that they can control with their everyday decisions.

87 In the News

The daily newspaper is an excellent resource for weaving the character thread throughout the fabric of the curriculum. The paper is filled with reading, writing, spelling, English, math, social studies, history, geography, and science-related stories. Just like life, the newspaper has it all.

While having your students search for a character-related story, you can have them look for compound subjects or predicates, adjectives and adverbs. You could have them circle all of the punctuation marks in the article. You could have them go on the prowl for all of the even numbers in a box score on the sports page. And when reading about famous people in the news, you can learn about the impact of good character throughout history. The list goes on!

The use of the newspaper is addressed in the homework section at the end of this book. Once you begin looking for ways to address curriculum concerns and skill mastery while meeting the character challenge, you will find more than you can use in any given school year. The rest, as they say, will be history.

88 The Daily News

A wonderful language arts activity that can incorporate character-teaching strategies is The Daily News. Near the end of the day, students brainstorm the day's events. The events are recorded on large chart paper by the teacher or by a student news reporter. Younger students sometimes like to dress up for the part. A sports coat and Clark Kent-type hat are always fun.

As the events are mentioned, the reporter writes the sentences down with a black marker. Then, depending on the skill you are trying to re-teach and reinforce, students are asked questions about the grammar, punctuation, and spelling of the sentences. Really simple concepts can be reinforced for younger students, such as periods, capital letters, and basic sight words. Older students can come to the chart and circle the direct object, the predicate, and the proper nouns. Use a different-color marker for each skill represented in your lesson.

It's a fun way to review skills and the events of the day will stay more clearly in the minds of the students as they leave for home. Perhaps when their parents ask what they did in school today, the answer just might be something other than "Nothing"!

89 Cross-Grade Tutoring

Planning for the academic success of your students doesn't always mean that you will deliver each and every lesson. Peer tutors are wonderful at getting the job done! My sixth graders are paired with younger students for two thirty-minute sessions each week. The reading teacher in our school prepares the lessons and the kids work well together towards mastery of skill. But although they are hard at work, they are also having fun together.

Some of the things we do together with our buddies include reading books and stories, practicing spelling words, practicing our handwriting on individual chalkboards, playing reading games, doing dictionary searches, writing poems, making booklets, and planning puppet shows and choral readings. The possibilities are endless with any subject matter!

These tutoring session helps build confidence, skill, and friendship. It is a help to the older students as well as to the younger ones. Both groups learn about good character by actually living the lessons we have taught in school. An added benefit to the older kids is that they begin to realize, firsthand, the power of modeling good behavior and character. They see how much the younger students look up to them and begin to feel the responsibility of good behavior at school—all day long. The benefits of these sessions go a long way toward making our school personally, as well as academically, stronger!

90 Ongoing Social Change

An important part of good citizenship is to value the aspects of social change that are needed in our communities and schools. The relevance to history is crucial. It is not enough to study the past and derive great lessons. We must learn to study current events in our country and world. Unfortunately, the attack on America on September 11, 2001, drives this point home! Since that terrible day, many classroom discussions in our social studies classes have hinged on that event. The kids have questions and concerns. We all do.

One way to keep abreast of the events in the news is to watch for cartoons in the newspaper. In the comic strips on Thanksgiving Day 2001, many of the artists devoted their strips to patriotic themes in remembrance of September 11. When I saw the touching tributes, I clipped them from the newspaper and ran copies for my students. We discussed each one in detail during our character and social studies classes and then glued them in our Character Journals.

Many times, editorial cartoons offer a glimpse of our world that even young children can understand. I run copies of these, too, and we follow the same format. It has been heartwarming, indeed, to see the children's response to these cartoons. They often will come in on Monday morning asking if there are any new cartoons to discuss and add to our journals. I believe that kids want to know about their world, and it empowers them to know that they can discuss the issues (if even in a simple way) and work towards social change.

These activities will help you and your students keep your finger on the pulse of our own history, as it is being written. Please don't miss out on the adventure!

91 Get On Board!

There will be times at your school when get the definite feeling that not every teacher is on board with the school's character mission. Some teachers will go all out and some will try just a few strategies. Remember that the comfort level is different for each of us. Rather than becoming discouraged, try to stay positive and know that we all cannot be the same. The key is to encourage, not to pressure. *All in good time* is wonderful wisdom!

But never underestimate the power of the character message. Once planted, the seeds will bloom in their own time and place. Know, too, that the students will do much to spread the enthusiasm of the message. Remember the words of Aesop: *Little by little does the trick!* Teaching for character translates academically. That we know. You can't hide it. Once teachers try a character strategy and get a taste of success, they will try more and more strategies for building climate and curriculum through the character message. It will begin an upward spiral of trying and buying in. Before long, you will see more and more teachers, students, and parents get on board!

The good news is... Teaching for character translates academically!

92 The Meaning of Character

As the year draws to an end, I like to do some kind of informal evaluation of how much my students have learned. This year I developed an assignment that I called *The Meaning of Character*. It took the students about four days to complete the assignment. I gave it to them during the last week of school when they were tired of listening and ready for summer to commence. Even though they were restless, I wanted to engage them in meaningful work. On this assignment they could work alone, with a partner, or in a group of three. The choice was theirs. I explained the assignment, put on some classical music, and then left them alone to think and to write. I just walked around the room and watched them work.

> "We have committed the Golden Rule to memory; let us now commit it to life."
>
> —Edwin Markam

There were four pages of character words: values, virtues, respect, responsibility, caring, fairness, citizenship, perseverance, integrity, trustworthiness, accountability, work ethic, compassion and character messenger. The students had to look up each word in the dictionary, discuss it and record the meaning. They also had to discuss and record an example of that trait in action. Their responses were grand, but I think the real value in the assignment was in discovering what they had already learned over the course of the year. I really enjoyed listening in on their discussions and reading their papers. Here is a sample of what they wrote.

Values	*something, as in a belief that is valuable or desirable* A desirable belief that is very powerful is believing in the Golden Rule.
Virtues	*conduct that agrees with what is morally right* I like to do the right thing!
Integrity	*total honesty and sincerity* I can be counted on to tell the truth. I am honest even when it is hard to be.
Work Ethic	*how well someone tries to do his job* Larry Bird has a good work ethic. He always tries his very best!
Character Messenger	*someone who tells others about character and the Golden Rule* Ms. Brown is a character messenger. We are *all* character messengers!

93 Family Character Night

This is one idea that actually came from a sixth-grade student named Wesley. It is one of my very favorites.

At our school, we have a Family Math Night and a Family Reading Night each school year. It is a fun night of friendship and learning. There is also a lot of food there and the families come for dinner first. After dinner, we have three half-hour sessions where families rotate for sessions. Teachers do the modeling for the learning games, then the kids and their parents set to work. It is heartwarming to see the parents interact with their children and it helps the teachers get to know the families, as well.

After one such evening, one of my sixth-grade students asked why we couldn't have a Character Class for parents. He thought it would be a grand idea! "Then they could learn all of the character lessons, too," Wesley, the student, told me. And so I brought up the idea with the principal and staff of our school. They all thought it would be a wonderful way to get the character message out into our school community and homes.

So we started brainstorming ideas. We planned the food agenda, a most inviting part of the evening. Then we gathered door prizes for the event. We bought a dozen of the best books on character and parenting to give away. *Parents, Kids, and Character* by Dr. Helen LeGette is the perfect book for every family! We also rounded up coupons for free pizza, hamburgers, ice cream, and milkshakes from our community fast-food restaurants.

The teachers planned the activities that would be presented that evening and we all signed up to help in some way. Some of us were actual presenters of a character message and activity. Some helped with registration and door prizes. Some helped with food and the clean-up committee. There were jobs for all of us!

This event is a worthwhile endeavor for any school. There are as many ideas for this type of evening as there are teachers in the world. But one aspect of our Family Character Night is a *must*. Kids cannot come alone to this event. To be admitted, they must bring at least one adult in their family. That is the key. That is the reason for the evening and the reason that this activity is so successful. So start planning now. Please don't miss out on a wonderful evening.

94 Student Planners

In our school, we plan for success. One of the best ways to do that is to purchase student assignment books or student planners. There are several types on the market to choose from. Our school has used several different types and has made revisions in our selection over the years. An important component that we look for is the layout of the book and the supporting *lessons* that are incorporated into each page. Mini-lessons, quotes and tips about the importance of attitude, decisions, and habits are so crucial to student success. One company now has a 32-page character education insert in its elementary, middle, and high school planners. What a wonderful addition to help students learn the necessary life skills that will help them meet with personal and academic success!

95 Tell the Principal

One of the best academic boosters in our school is a trip to the principal's office. Mr. Handley loves to celebrate the successes of his students! Years ago, he had a special stamp made. It is large and round and has the special seal and logo for our school. It is quite impressive. Kids love to have their papers stamped. And of course, Mr. Handley loves it, too!

Whenever a student scores a good grade on a test or makes progress after struggling with a certain skill or academic concept, he gets to go and tell the principal. It is heartwarming, indeed, to watch a student skip out of the classroom door on his or her way to the office. Mr. Handley takes the time to talk with each and every student, to congratulate them and recognize the effort that was made. He always ties in the character message with each of those talks with kids. He then lets them reach into his large pencil jar for the icing on the proverbial cake. I can assure you, this strategy goes a long way in developing the academic and character climate of our school!

96 The Affirmation Handshake

This is another of Mr. Handley's specialties. The teachers in our school take the time to fill the principal in on student progress. Sometimes it is just as simple as a student breaking the tardiness habit by coming to school on time. It could be that a struggling student makes progress with turning in homework or better listening in class. Whatever the reason, we feel it is *cause for applause.* Noticing these benchmarks in a student's academic journey is the first step. Appreciating them is the next. But for the student, the affirmation is the motivating factor that makes him want to continue on the right path.

> For the student, the affirmation is the motivating factor that makes him want to continue on the right path.

Mr. Handley keeps all of our student comments in the forefront of his mind. At some time during the school day, he will intentionally seek out the child. He may pass the student in the hallway or catch up with him as he is waiting in the cafeteria line. Mr. Handley simply walks up to the student and extends his hand for an affirmation handshake. He looks the student right in the eye and smiles. He then gives the well-deserved compliment. The look on the child's face is priceless! This kind of appreciation and affirmation from the principal is powerful in securing additional effort on the part of the students. I have seen that handshake turn a slipping child around and set him back on the road to success!

97 One More Step

When students turn in an assignment and you have graded their effort, make a personal comment on how that student can take one more step toward academic excellence. Just marking things wrong will not do the trick. Marking things right—and then elaborating on the suggested next step—will give students the motivation, inspiration and direction they need. It takes so little time to do, but these written comments develop academic integrity in amazing ways.

> Remember...in our complex technological lives, the most important element in teaching is still the human element.

The direction you provide does not need to be in written form. A personal comment in verbal form is powerful, too. Just pulling a student aside, walking beside him to the cafeteria or gym, or catching him before he boards the bus to go home are all opportunities for a directional comment or suggestion. Kids can tell when teachers are sincerely interested in them. They respond with the effort and extra work that makes you proud!

Remember that in our complex technological lives, the most important element in teaching is still the *human* element. That is the one thing that will make all of the difference in the curriculum that you provide your students!

98 Would-Works

Over the course of your teaching career, you will have tried many things in an effort to help your students achieve academic and personal excellence. Every year the kids are different, so every year we have to try new things. By tuning in to kids, we can find what it is that we can do to motivate, inspire, and lead. That is the true calling of a teacher. Through trial and error, we stumble upon ways that work for our students.

About ten years into my teaching career, I began documenting the practices that work best. Fifteen years later, I have quite a collection. These ideas, which I call *would-works*, are cherished, reread, and studied by me often. What works with one student will not always work with others. Each year each class and each student is different, so it pays to have a large bag of tricks to pull from!

My suggestion to you is to begin now. Take a few minutes to write down the things that you have found that work with your students. Keep the documentation going all school year long. Keep copies of student work to help jog your memory. I always ask permission from students to copy their work and have always found them to be quite gracious and accommodating. Sometimes I keep a copy of a lesson plan or a semantic map that we have made in class. If a bulletin board is the example that you want to remember, just snap a picture of it. Collect any keepsake that will make the point long after the school year has ended. And before you know it, you will have your own collection of *Would-Works* that will support you in your career working with kids!

99 Thank-You Books

There are times throughout the school year when you need for your students to thank those who have helped your class in some way. This may be a parent volunteer, a resource person who comes to share a lesson with your class, or a person you visited on a class field trip. Whatever the reason, it is important that you demonstrate the respect and gratitude aspects of good character. It is for these occasions that our class always makes a thank-you book.

It takes just a few minutes of your day and the activity can be woven into the instructional strategies and goals in your lesson plans. Each student writes a letter of thanks for the good deed that was done. I also ask students to decorate their letter with artwork to make it more personal and attractive. When students turn in their letters, we put them in a colorful folder that also includes a personal note from the teacher.

I also include a few snapshots of the volunteer or resource people helping us with our lesson or activity. It makes for a really nice thank-you gift. From start to finish, this activity takes about thirty minutes. We put on the music and set to work! The children enjoy writing the letters and doing the artwork. I just write it into my language arts and art lesson plans as an integrated lesson. We send off the folder, knowing that it will make a statement about the kind of class we are trying to be. It is not enough to simply learn the character message, it is important to live it, as well. Sending thank-you books into the community is a wonderful way to spread the character message all over town!

PART 3

The Support

Character Messages
for students to take home
in their backpacks

The Homework Connection
Activities for students and their families

Here they are! Homework ideas to send home in the backpacks of your students, with one activity for each week of the school year. Perhaps you will consider making a certain night of the week *Character Homework Night*. It's an easy way to develop the consistent expectation and habit at home. Families will come to look forward to these learning and bonding experiences when the character message finds its way home in the backpack!

There several types of activities included:

- **Activity Sheets**—*ready to run copies of character lessons*

- **Defining Character**—*can be used over and over again during the course of the school year by simply changing the character trait to be studied*

- **Read and Discuss**—*thought-provoking lessons and stories to read and discuss at home*

- **In the News**—*can be used several times during the school year to help students tie-in current events and character*

Of course, there are as many different ways to approach these character assignments as there are teachers and classrooms. I recommend discussing the assignment before sending it home. Then follow up the next day by discussing the assignment in class. I have witnessed some wonderful learning by taking class time for student sharing! Just remember, the important thing is not *how* you do the homework assignments with your kids. The important thing is *that* you do it!

There's no magic wand to developing good character. **It takes work!**

Every day you need to make good decisions and good choices. Here's how:

THINK IT OVER.
THINK IT THROUGH.
DECIDE WHAT'S REALLY BEST FOR YOU!

> # 1. Think   2. Decide   3. Do!

Use the examples below as practice for making good decisions. After thinking it over, circle your decision.

I don't feel like listening to the teacher. I think I'll just draw for a bit instead.   Yes   No

The teacher gave too much homework. I think I'll just do part of it.   Yes   No

My friend asks me if he can copy my homework. I don't think we'll get caught.   Yes   No

I'm late for soccer practice. It won't matter that my homework is sloppy.   Yes   No

"Don't do what's easy...do what's right!"
—Maw Great

Keep pecking away!

How many times does a woodpecker peck at the bark of a tree while he is looking for food?

1 time?   10 times?   100 times?

The answer is: **Until he gets the job done!**

The woodpecker's very life depends upon his work ethic.

Your success in school depends upon your work habits.
When you have an assignment to do, remember the woodpecker...and keep pecking away until *your* job is done!

Check the tasks that will help you get your homework finished:

___ Find a quiet place to study   ___ Take pride in your work

___ Turn off the T.V.   ___ Take your book home

___ Do part of the assignment   ___ Write down assignments

___ Leave your books at school   ___ Think of your report card

___ Talk on the phone   ___ Have a friend over

___ Write as fast as you can   ___ Wait until the last minute

___ Close your bedroom door   ___ Remember your goals

"There is nothing that cannot be achieved by firm determination."

—Japanese proverb

Stock your toolbox!

Every student needs to stock his own personal toolbox with good character traits and habits. These will help you become successful at everything you do. So when you have a job to do, reach for the right tools!

Match the character trait with the habit it represents:

___ **Responsibility**   A. Listening when the teacher is talking

___ **Trustworthiness**   B. Working at it until you get it right

___ **Caring**   C. Being able to be counted on

___ **Work Ethic**   D. Treating all classmates the same

___ **Citizenship**   E. Completing all assignments

___ **Respect**   F. Helping a friend who falls down

___ **Dependability**   G. Doing good deeds in the community

___ **Fairness**   H. Never cheating on a test

___ **Perseverance**   I. Always trying your best

List the tools that you will put in your own personal toolbox:

_____

_____

_____

_____

_____

"Dream, plan...build!"

—**Deb Austin Brown**

Good character is so bright you'll need shades!

Talk about these character traits with your family.

Discuss the meaning of each trait.

Discuss when you have seen these in action in your family and home.

Make plans to work towards these characteristics as goals!

Respect **Responsibility**

Honesty Integrity Self-Control

Caring *Kindness* **Citizenship**

"Look for the best in others...
and in yourself!"

—Deb Austin Brown

Pump yourself up...
with good character!

Just like an athlete training for strength, it takes daily practice to become strong in character. Pump yourself up with good character by discussing these traits with your family and by practicing these habits at home. Report back on at least one each week for the coming month.

- Being kind to your classmates and family
- Telling the truth to your teacher and parents
- Doing your best in school
- Thinking things through
- Making good decisions
- Studying for tests
- Doing your homework
- Doing your chores at home without being told
- Showing compassion and cooperation on the homefront

"There are no shortcuts
to any place worth going."

—Beverly Sills

Measure Up to your full potential!

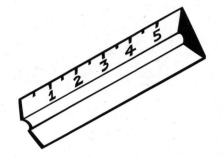

By setting goals, you can begin measuring up to your full potential in life. Use the goal-setting sheet below to fill in some of your personal and academic goals. After discussing your goals with your family, bring the list to school to share with the class. Keep your list close by so that you can refer to it each day. Research proves that you will achieve more by *writing* down your goals and working towards them! So get out your pencil and get going!

Personal Goals

1._____

2._____

3._____

Academic Goals

1._____

2._____

3._____

Target practice helps!

Put your personal and academic goals on the target below...and start practicing!

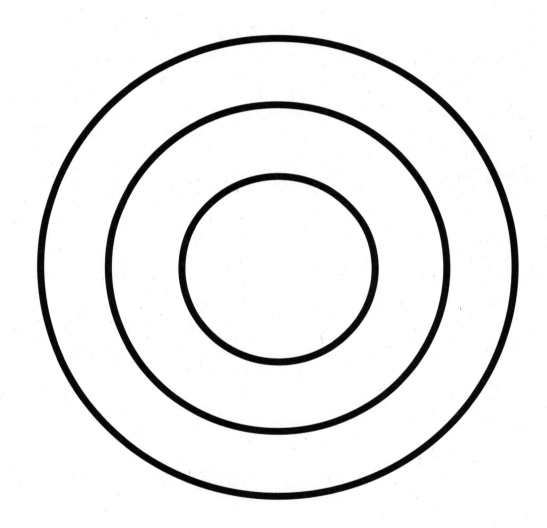

"You miss 100% of the shots you never take!"

—Wayne Gretzsky

Run through open doors
of opportunity!

An open door is very inviting! It always poses as an opportunity in disguise. Once we take a step through a door, a new world is opened to us! For example, a friend invites us to a basketball game. It is the opportunity to meet new people and perhaps to play a new sport. Or a teacher tells you that he thinks you have a knack for writing poetry. That is an open door to exploring your potential as a writer.

Think of some doors that have opened for you recently. Write down what it was and the new opportunity that was presented. Then write down what you intend to do about the new world of possibilities in your life! And the next time that a new door opens for you, don't just walk through that door...run!

Door #1	Door #2	Door #3	Door #4

Picture it!

Picture yourself as a kid of character!

You can become the person of your dreams! With hard work and a good character ethic, the possibilities are endless! Close your eyes and see yourself the way you would like to be. Then imagine *your* picture in a frame hanging in the school hallway. What would you like for the caption to read? How would you want to be remembered?

Draw yourself in the picture frame below and write a caption describing your character... the way you want to be remembered!

Think about good character!

Sometimes good character is just a thought away! Taking time to think things through will help you to make good decisions that will build up your character. Do it now!

Take the time to think about some good things that you can do to make yourself a better person and to make the world a better place. Write them down so that you can discuss them with your family this evening and with your classmates at school tomorrow!

Good Ideas for Character!

1. _____

2. _____

3. _____

4. _____

5. _____

6. _____

7. _____

Get excited
about doing
the right thing!

Good things make the world come alive with excitement!

Think of some times when you got excited about something new and good in your life! Write them down and talk about them with your family and friends at school. Discuss how goodness is contagious and fills the earth with a sense of excitement!

1. _____
2. _____
3. _____
4. _____
5. _____

Now make a plan to get excited about doing more good things!

1. _____
2. _____
3. _____

Let your character shine!

Never let the light of your good character be hidden. Let it shine! It has a way of making the world a better place for all of us!

Do the matching exercise below to help you think about and understand how one good deed, one act of kindness, can shine out into the world, making it a better place. Then, talk about this with your family and classmates. Keep this sheet as a reminder to try a few of the suggestions yourself!

Matching

A. Listening to a friend

B. Honoring a confidence

C. Helping with a problem

D. Lending a book

E. Smiling at people

F. Helping with a chore

G. Being kind

H. Giving a compliment

I. Doing a favor

J. Giving encouragement

___ makes you feel better!

___ makes the world better!

___ builds character!

___ is uplifting!

___ makes you smile!

___ makes someone's day!

___ makes a difference!

___ really helps out!

___ really counts!

___ is contagious!

Get the character habit!

It all starts with your attitude! That positive or negative attitude will determine the decisions that you make. Those decisions will lead to habits in your life. Those habits determine your character! Good decisions and habits will make for a wonderful life, while bad decisions and habits will help you reap a garden of weeds.

Take some time to list some of the good habits that you would like to cultivate in your life. Now get busy sowing the seeds!

Good habits that I would like to have:

1. _____

2. _____

3. _____

4. _____

5. _____

Now discuss with your family the ways that you can cultivate these habits so that they can become part of your character!

Look for the best... in you!

In the mirror below, write down some of your best character traits.

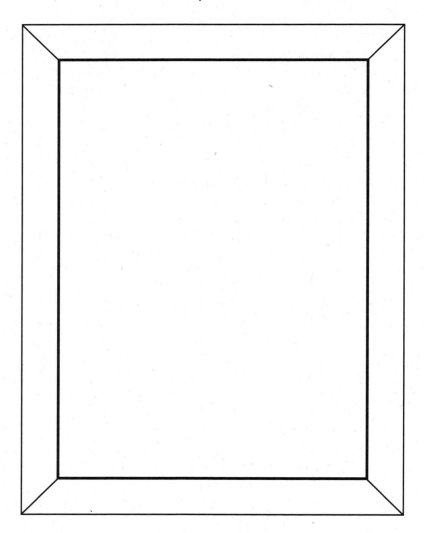

If you have difficulty seeing the best in yourself, ask someone in your family for ideas.

Looking for the best in yourself will help you to develop the habit of looking for the best in others!

A + B = C
Attitudes + Behavior = Character

The equation is simple!

Below are listed a few equations to help get you started. Then let the brainstorming begin!

Think about, talk about, and write down a few equations of your own. Be prepared to write your favorite on the chalkboard at school tomorrow!

Positive attitude + Cooperation = Teamwork

Cheerful disposition + Effort = The job done!

Responsibility + Hard work = Good grades

_____ + _____ = _____

_____ + _____ = _____

_____ + _____ = _____

_____ + _____ = _____

_____ + _____ = _____

_____ + _____ = _____

Each day
is a clean slate!

We all make mistakes. They are a necessary part of life because we can learn from them!

On the clean slate below, write down a few recent mistakes...and what you learned from each one.

Now, take the pretend eraser and wipe your slate clean!

Read
and discuss

As a family, read the lesson together and spend some time talking about it. Be prepared to share your insights in class.

The Company You Keep

You are judged by the company you keep. Kids for generations have been raised on this proverbial wisdom. And whether or not it is fair, this axiom is certainly true!

In life, we choose our friends by their values. We almost always want and choose friends that complement our lives, our decisions, and our beliefs. Rarely do we choose friends who stand for things that we don't believe in.

Friendships tend to thrive when we become comfortable with others because our values and our beliefs mesh. Our best friends encourage us to be good and they bring out the best in us!

Relationships that breed problems are not friendships at all. These relationships foster bad decisions. They often lead us down less-than-honorable pathways in life. So when choosing friends, remember that you will be judged by the company that you keep. Choose honorable friends or none at all. Stand up for what is right...even if you are standing alone!

Read and discuss

As a family, read the lesson together and spend some time talking about it. Be prepared to share your insights in class.

Is It a Good Trade?

How do your children spend their free time when school is not in session? The answer to this question will give great insight into the kind of student and person your child will become!

Many kids spend most of their free time watching television and movies, playing video and computer games, and listening to music. Many of the shows, movies, games, and lyrics contain disrespect, adult situations, bad language, and violence. These messages run counter to the character message that we teach in school. These messages—however subtle—teach kids to take life's *lower* road.

After your child's entertainment-time, help your child to reflect with a little self-talk: *I have just traded an hour of my life to do this activity. Was it a good trade? Did it help me with my goal of becoming a better student and a better person?*

If so, then tune in to this kind of show or entertainment more often. If not, then perhaps a change of habits is in order. Remember, the messages that we give our children—by design or default—will stay with them for their entire lives!

Read and discuss

As a family, read the lesson together and spend some time talking about it. Be prepared to share your insights in class.

Respect Is a Two-Way Street

Our school is a *Golden Rule School*. From the moment that students walk into the building until the moment they leave on the school bus at the end of the day, the character message is a part of all that we do.

The Golden Rule is about treating others the way that you would like to be treated. This rule applies to teachers as well as students. All teachers work hard to apply the Golden Rule to their own lives and to their own classrooms. The result is that respect is modeled, taught, and learned each day.

At home, the Golden Rule is the best rule! Parents simply cannot expect their children to show respect if it is not modeled in the home. Parents who yell and scream, fuss and hit—and then expect respect in return—send conflicting and confusing messages to their children.

Respect is a two-way street. When parents give respect, they often get it in return. So, give it...and get it! It's a great way to live in any home!

Read and discuss

As a family, read the lesson together and spend some time talking about it. Be prepared to share your insights in class.

A Good Intellect and a Good Heart

The ancient writings of Aristotle and Socrates hold wisdom and insight into the power and importance of teaching for character. The combined teachings of these Greek philosophers tell us that we should lead children to know, love, and do the good in life.

Aristotle, especially, taught that repetition is the mother of skill. He believed that when students have the opportunity to practice the good, they will come to develop good habits. And as we know, our habits and decisions define the kind of students and people that we become.

Along with Aristotle, our school believes that we can help children develop a good intellect and a good heart. Intellectual excellence and personal excellence must be developed together over the course of a lifetime. Teaching begins in the home and must certainly continue throughout the schooling of a child. And of course, intellectual and character development are most effective when the home, school and community all work together for the child in an intentional and consistent way.

What can we all do to work towards this important goal?

Read and discuss

As a family, read the lesson together and spend some time talking about it. Be prepared to share your insights in class.

The Common Good

Thinking about others is an important part of living. Responding to others is what we call good citizenship. Citizenship is belonging. We all belong to neighborhoods, schools, churches, cities, states, and to the United States. In order to be good citizens, we must give of ourselves to contribute to the common good of our communities. It is our duty to be good citizens, to do good works for the common good.

Our Constitution has given us rights, but with rights come responsibilities. Freedom has its price. The September 11, 2001, attack on America has shown the importance of answering the call of citizenship. In big ways and small ways, we find citizens giving of themselves for the common good. It is heartwarming to see!

We need to show good citizenship at all times, not just during a crisis. Contributing for the common good of our schools and communities should be a daily habit. It should become a way of life!

It is an honor and a duty to be an American. Let's all work together for the common good...every day!

Read and discuss

As a family, read the lesson together and spend some time talking about it. Be prepared to share your insights in class.

The Benefit of the Doubt

As a new school year gets under way, you need to know that there is a wonderful gift that we can all give others in our school community. This beautiful and appreciated gift is called the *benefit of the doubt*. Often it seems like a common, ordinary thing. But giving someone the benefit of the doubt is a rare and wonderful occurrence in today's world.

Often in our daily interactions with people, we jump to conclusions, make assumptions, give in to gossip, and make premature judgments. Many times, these judgments are unfair and inaccurate. This causes us to make mountains out of molehills and then problems begin to grow, blowing things out of proportion.

Giving someone the benefit of the doubt is a gift that teachers and students can give each other. It promotes understanding and it bonds them together in a powerful way!

It can also be a gift that parents and teachers share. This means that they will listen to each other in respectful ways that will result in good communication. And we all know that the better the communication is between home and school, the better education becomes for kids!

Read
and discuss

As a family, read the lesson together and spend some time talking about it. Be prepared to share your insights in class.

The Power of Words

Words mean something. Words are powerful in communicating our thoughts and feelings to others. We need to choose our words wisely, especially when dealing with children. The bad news is that words can *tear down*. They can be insulting, harsh, humiliating, pejorative, critical, demeaning, shaming, or degrading. They can hurt a child and break his or her spirit. The scars can be long lasting.

But the good news is, words can *build up!* They can be encouraging, uplifting, expecting, inspiring, motivating, comforting, and understanding. They can make a difference in every child's life.

It is important to try to choose our words wisely. If we are successful, the results will be positively uplifting!

Read and discuss

As a family, read the lesson together and spend some time talking about it. Be prepared to share your insights in class.

Resolve To Be Positive!

With the start of a new year on the horizon, it's a good time to think about resolutions. Historically, the beginning of the new year is the time reserved for a little introspection and reflection. It's the perfect time to address the less-than-perfect areas of our lives.

In life, there are so many issues over which we have no control. What we can choose to control is our reaction and response to those things. We can choose to see life's glass as half empty or half full. In other words, we can choose to be negative or positive.

A positive attitude is the foundation for a happy life! We can't have a bad day with a positive attitude, nor can we have a good day if we choose to see things in a negative light. The choice really is ours!

The new year is on the horizon. We will sail through the new year facing all of the wonderful opportunities and challenges that wait ahead on the seas of life. How will we navigate these uncertain waters? How will we choose to see the journey ahead?

Attitude really is a choice! As you sail through the new year, what kind of sailor will you be? What attitude will you choose as your lens for looking at the world? Resolve to be positive! It will help keep your ship on a more even keel. Look for the joy in the new year. With a positive attitude, you will find it!

Read and discuss

As a family, read the lesson together and spend some time talking about it. Be prepared to share your insights in class.

The Gift of Words

As the holiday season approaches, we are all busier than ever. We have so much to do in such a little time. Tensions mount as the stress of the season becomes more familiar with each passing day.

In an effort to find *just the right gift* to give family and friends, we often overlook simple gifts. Simple gifts are real treasures! They are the everyday gestures and gifts that we can give to others—gifts that cost nothing, but reap great rewards.

A smile, a pat on the back, simple encouragement, and a sincere compliment are simple gifts that brighten our days. Mark Twain once wrote, "I can go for two months on a good compliment." What wisdom!

Words can be encouraging, praising, uplifting, motivational, and inspiring! Please take time to give others the gift of words. It could be the *best* gift of the season!

Read and discuss

As a family, read the lesson together and spend some time talking about it. Be prepared to share your insights in class.

Get the Character Habit!

Habits are powerful in defining our lives and charting our destiny. Harvard and Stanford research shows that 90% to 95% of what we do each day is attributed to habit. This statistic shows how habits that might begin as spontaneous actions in our lives grow into cables that chain us to our behaviors!

Many of us end up learning the powerful lesson on habits the hard way. We spontaneously act in a certain way and then we begin to grow comfortable with the behavior. The longer this behavior is a part of our lives, the more difficult it will be to change.

Will we consciously choose to cultivate the homework habit, or will we spend our time making excuses for not doing it? Will we develop the habit of getting up on time for school and getting there before the tardy bell, or will we get the late-for-school habit? Will we deliberately choose to work to our true potential, thus developing the habit of a good work ethic, or will we chain ourselves to the habit of just getting by?

We have to remember that the choice is ours. We can intentionally choose to develop good habits that will serve us well, or we can incidentally acquire bad habits that we will spend considerable time and effort trying to break. We make our decision with each and every choice we make, each and every day. The best choice of all? Get the character habit!

In the news!

For this evening's assignment, take a look through the daily newspaper. If a paper is not available, turn on a segment of the television news. Watch for a story that exemplifies good or bad character. Cut out the news article or take notes on the news clip. Then, answer the following questions. Bring the story and your answers with you to school tomorrow.

News Story: _____

News Source: _____

1. What is this story mainly about?

2. What are the character traits that are illustrated in the story?

3. Rewards: How did good character help?

4. Consequences: How did bad character hurt?

5. What life-lessons could be learned from this news story?

Would-Works!

Take some time to think about, ask others, and decide on some ideas that would work to help you do better in school and at home. After you figure them out, write them down below. Put them in your backpack so we can discuss them at school tomorrow!

Ideas That Would Work at School

1. _____

2. _____

3. _____

4. _____

5. _____

Ideas That Would Work at Home

1. _____

2. _____

3. _____

4. _____

5. _____

Groundbreaking projects!

Take some think-time to reflect on some things that you would like to do, goals that you would like to achieve, and projects that you would like to get off the ground!

Now write down your plans! Talk about them with a family member, and then bring them to school to share with your classmates.

Dreams, Projects, and Goals

1. _____

2. _____

3. _____

4. _____

5. _____

6. _____

7. _____

8. _____

9. _____

10. _____

Blueprint for success!

Just like an architect who is designing a plan, you need to construct your own blueprint for success.

Take some time to design your own plan for turning negative behaviors into positive ones! A few examples are given just to get you started. Now try a few of your own!

Negatives	Positives
Complaining about chores	Doing chores with a smile
Hitting my brother	Showing kindness
Keeping a messy room	Getting organized
Making homework excuses	Doing my homework
Talking during class	Staying on task

Defining character

Character Trait: _____

Tonight for homework, ask three people what this character trait means to them. Write their responses in the appropriate places. Then think about what you have learned about this trait. Come up with your own definition!

1. _____
   _____

2. _____
   _____

3. _____
   _____

My own definition:

_____
_____
_____

443 character quotes and words of wisdom...

Use these quotes on the morning announcements, for student Character Journals, in school newsletters, on school walls and posters, and on your school marquee.

"Don't do what's easy...do what's right!"   —Maw Great

Be in the right place, at the right time, doing the right thing.

There are two ways to get to the top of an oak tree. You can climb the branches, or you can sit on an acorn and wait.

"Winning is a habit. Unfortunately, so is losing."   —Vince Lombardi

"Character is a by-product. It is produced in the great manufacture of daily duty."   —Woodrow Wilson

"If I take care of my character, my reputation will take care of itself."
—Dwight L. Moody

"Moral excellence comes about as a result of habit. We become just by doing just acts, temperate by doing temperate acts, brave by doing brave acts."
—Aristotle

"You cannot dream yourself into character; you must hammer and forge yourself one."   —James A. Froude

"In truth, the only difference between those who have failed and those who have succeeded lies in the difference of their habits."   —Og Mandino

"We first make our habits, and then our habits make us."   —John Dryden

"Every man is the architect of his own character."   —G. D. Boardman

"Character isn't inherited. One builds it daily by the way one thinks and acts—thought by thought, action by action."   —Helen G. Douglas

"There is nothing so fatal to character as half-finished tasks."   —David Lloyd

Whatever your lot in life, build something on it.

"Character consists of what you do on the third and fourth tries."
—James A. Michener

"He who stops being better stops being good." —Oliver Cromwell

People may doubt what you say, but they will believe what you do.

"Do all the good you can, by all the means you can, in all the ways you can, in all the places you can, at all the times you can, to all the people you can, as long as ever you can." —John Wesley

"Some people strengthen the society just by being the kind of people they are." —John W. Gardener

"Always do right. This will gratify most people and astonish the rest." —Mark Twain

"America was built not by politicians running for something, but by statesmen standing for something." —Vance Havner

The greatest hope of society is individual character.

"Character building begins in our infancy and continues until death." —Eleanor Roosevelt

Fads come and go; wisdom and character go on forever.

"Character is long-standing habit." —Plutarch

"Truthfulness is a cornerstone in character, and if it be not firmly laid in youth, there will ever be a weak spot in the foundation." —Jefferson Davis

"He who always gives way to others will end up having no principles of his own." —Aesop

A bad attitude is like a flat tire, you can't go anywhere until you change it.

You don't have to attend every argument that you're invited to.

You can't talk you way out of something that you've already behaved your way into.

"Our decisions define us." —Deb Austin Brown

"I think I can...I know I can!" —The Little Engine That Could

Kids go where there is excitement, they stay where there is love.

No matter how far you have gone down a wrong road, turn back.

If you are planning to go no where, just follow the crowd.

"Today's students can put dope in their veins or hope in their brains." —Jesse Jackson

"It is not your aptitude but your attitude that will determine your altitude."

—Jesse Jackson

When things go wrong, don't go with them.

Light tomorrow with today.

You are not old until you have lost all of your marvels.

"You miss 100% of the shots you never take."

—Wayne Gretzsky

"Teamwork is the best work."

—Deb Austin Brown

Every day is a good day. You need to make it a good day for you!

"Doing your best at this moment puts you in the best place for the next moment."

—Oprah Winfrey

"You can't build a reputation on what you are going to do."

—Henry Ford

"People forget how fast you did a job, but they remember how well you did it."

—Howard W. Newton

"Know the good, love the good, do the good."

—Aristotle/Socrates/Lickona

"Developing good character isn't easy. There is no magic wand. It takes work!"

—Deb Austin Brown

"Where have all the heroes gone?"

—Senator Robert Byrd, West Virginia

Waste of time is the most extravagant and costly of all expenses.

"It is through cooperation, rather than conflict, from which your greatest successes will be derived."

—Ralph Charell

The pleasure that you get from life is equal to the attitude that you put into it.

"Count your blessings by name."

—William Mitchell

It doesn't do any good to sit up and take notice, if you just keep sitting.

"Just tell the truth. It will save you every time."

—Oprah Winfrey

If you want to build character, start now!

Good grades are something you have to achieve, not something that is free to receive.

Never settle for less than your best!

Ask people's advice, but decide for yourself.

Pride is a personal commitment. It is an attitude that separates excellence from mediocrity.

Every day, go out of your way to do something kind.

Our past is not our potential.

"It is always too soon to quit."   —*Norman Vincent Peale*

If you don't try, you won't know. If you don't know, you won't grow.

"A determined person allows no exceptions to success. Exceptions tear down a success habit faster than victories can build it up."   —*Sterling W. Sill*

Don't just do it...do it right!

What is popular is not always right. What is right is not always popular.

Positive people don't blame others for their mistakes.

The one thing worse than a quitter is the person who is afraid to begin.

"Always follow through. Stopping at third base doesn't add any more to the score than striking out."   —*Babe Ruth*

Getting something done is an accomplishment. Getting something done well is an achievement.

Doing little things well is a step toward doing big things better.

"Virtually nothing on earth can stop a person with a positive attitude who has his goal clearly in sight."   —*Denis Waitley*

"The best prize life offers is the chance to work hard at work worth doing."   —*Theodore Roosevelt*

You can't have a good day with a bad attitude, and you can't have a bad day with a good attitude!

Fly like the wind, reach for the stars...and you will shine like the sun!

"I will study and prepare...and someday my chance will come."   —*Abraham Lincoln*

"How many children are discouraged from pursuing an education because teachers have taken it upon themselves to judge who can achieve and who cannot? I wasn't there to judge my students. My job as a teacher was to get their talents working. And that's what I tried to do."   —*Marva Collins*

Don't settle for average. It's as close to the bottom as it is to the top.

The key to a good memory is to pay attention in the first place.

"If you think you can do a thing or think you can't do a thing, you're right."
—Henry Ford

"It is better to be alone that to be in bad company." —George Washington

"With ordinary talent and extraordinary perseverance, all things are attainable."
—T.F. Buxton

When things happen that you don't like, you have two choices: you can get bitter or you can get better.

"The best way to have a friend is to be a friend." —Ralph Waldo Emerson

If you can't say anything nice, don't say anything at all.

Optimists are people who take the cold water thrown at them, heat it with enthusiasm, and use the steam to push ahead.

Can't means you won't.

Everything you need for a happy life is within yourself.

"When everything seems to be going against you, remember that the airplane takes off against the wind—not with it." —Henry Ford

Everything you think affects your attitude, your mind, and your spirit. So think positively!

The best way to predict your future is to create it with goals and hard work.

"The secret of getting ahead is getting started." —Sally Berger

"Never, ever let anyone convince you to take drugs. If you do, you not only destroy your self-respect, but your dreams as well." —Marvin Hamlisch

"I'll tell you the same thing my mother used to tell me: The most important thing in life is to try to do the very best for your neighbors. Respect other people." —Hank Aaron

"Love yourself. Respect yourself. Never sell yourself short. Believe in yourself regardless of what people think. You can accomplish anything—absolutely anything—if you set your mind to it." —Marcus Allen

"Shoot for the moon. For even if you don't make it, you will land among the stars." —Mary Kay Ash

"Virtue is not left to stand alone. He who practices it will have neighbors." —Confucius

"Little by little does the trick."

—*Aesop*

"A man's character is the sum of the principles and values that guide his actions in the face of moral choices."
—*Nathaniel Branden*

When it comes to grades, what goes up doesn't have to go down.

"Learn all you can about people in other parts of the world. Understanding how people in other countries live and work and play teaches us to respect them, and it promotes peace everywhere."
—*Carol Bellamy, Peace Corps Director*

"Stay busy with your life. Study hard, go to school, play sports, get a job. But don't just lie around doing nothing. That is when you find trouble to get into."
—*Bobby Bowden*

"You've got to pay attention to the fundamentals. You do have to work hard. You do have to study. You do have to pay attention to the real things in life. If you do just half of what your parents tell you, you'll probably be twice as far ahead."
—*Tom Brokaw*

"Truth is the only ground to stand upon."
—*Elizabeth Cady Stanton*

"In life you are given two ends—one to think with and one to sit on. Your success in life depends on which end you use most. Heads you win, tails you lose!"
—*Senator Conrad Burns, Montana*

"Obey your parents. Grow up to be strong. Stay out of the drug scene."
—*George Bush*

"Do everything the best you can. Everything. The key to success is to be the best you can possibly be at every task you encounter and every role you play. By doing this, you prepare yourself for every opportunity." —*Barbara Bush*

"Patriotism is not so much protecting the land of our fathers as preserving the land of our children."
—*Jose Ortega y Gasset*

"We must use time creatively, and forever realize that the time is always ripe to do right."
—*Martin Luther King, Jr.*

"I truly believe that our thoughts influence what we experience in life. Do yourself a favor, and spend at least one moment today thinking of our world as a safe, healthy, and wonderful place to be!"
—*LeVar Burton*

"Self-esteem is that deep-down inside-the-skin feeling you have of your own self-worth."
—*Denis Waitley*

"Do all the good you can, by all the means you can."
—*John Wesley*

"Life is not a goal, it is a process. You get there step by step." —*Leo Buscaglia*

"While you are in school, you will encounter learning opportunities that you may never have again. Enjoy them all and take advantage of them all! The future of our great nation will soon be in the hands of young people like you."
—*Jimmy Carter*

"Every now and then, without anyone knowing about it, do something kind for someone who needs it and doesn't expect it. Things like that circulate the earth in invisible ways and make this planet a better place."   —*Brett Butler*

"Know and take pride in your history and heritage so that your generation is able to make greater strides in the future."   —*Ben Nighthorse Campbell*

"Have the courage to stay with your own opinion."   —*David Caruso*

"The character ethic is the foundation of all true success and happiness."
—*Stephen Covey*

Don't confuse your net worth with your self-worth!

"Our rewards in life will always be in exact proportion to the amount of consideration we show towards others."   —*Earl Nightingale*

There is a great distance between *said* and *done*.   —*Puerto Rican Proverb*

Someday is not a day of the week.

"Great discoveries and improvements invariably involve the cooperation of many minds."   —*Alexander Graham Bell*

"Just don't give up trying to do what you really want to do. Where there's love and inspiration, I don't think you can go wrong."   —*Ella Fitzgerald*

Adversity is the best source of strength.   —*Japanese proverb*

When all else fails, try persistence.

"Whatever you want to do, do it now. There are only so many tomorrows."
—*Michael Landon*

"Good character is contagious. Pass it on to others."   —*Anonymous*

"If you have a clear conscience you can lie down and sleep anywhere. If you don't, not even a comfortable bed will help."   —*Jack Austin (Deb's dad)*

Let the choices you make today be choices you can live with tomorrow.

For success, attitude is as important as ability!

Stand up for what is right, even if you're standing alone.

You are the future. Do you like what you see?

Don't just make decisions, make good decisions!

When you believe in yourself, anything is possible!

No one is a failure who keeps on trying.

Be responsible. Actions have consequences.

Let your efforts rise above your excuses.

You can always be a better person today than the one you were yesterday.

Don't just do enough to get by—do enough to get ahead!

A tendency that has run through your family for generations can stop with you. You're a transition person—a link between the past and the future. The future can be anything you choose for it to be!

All things are difficult before they are easy.

"Work before play."

—Aesop

"Well done is better than well said."

—Benjamin Franklin

"Decide on a challenging goal, something you would really like to do in your life—then work hard to reach it. Don't let the fear of failure hold you back. It is not a tragedy to strive for something and not achieve it. It is a tragedy to never try."

—Rosalynn Carter

Never take the easy way out.

"Nothing is more important for the public welfare than to form and train our youth in wisdom and virtue."

—Benjamin Franklin

"An error means a child needs help, not a reprimand or ridicule for doing something wrong."

—Marva Collins

"How far you go in life depends on your being tender with the young, compassionate with the aged, sympathetic with the striving, and tolerant of the weak and strong. Because someday in life you will have been all of these."

—George Washington Carver

"Keep your feet on the ground, your nose to the grindstone, and your eye on the sky!"

—Phyllis Diller

"Make sure you get an education. Do what's right in school. Listen to your teachers. You know what to do!"

—Joe DiMaggio

"Hold a true friend with both your hands."

—Nigerian proverb

"To make it easy to follow all the rules, follow the Golden Rule!"

—Zack, age 12

"Be cool...and follow the rules!" —*Casey, age 12*

"Making the A Honor Roll: You have to work hard. It feels good!"
—*Cody, age 12*

"Bad character is like a rock that sinks. Good character is like a boat that floats." —*Lucas, age 12*

"Bad habits put holes in your boat." —*Chris, age 12*

"If your path is dark, light it up with good character!" —*Daya, age 12*

"Don't fight, do what's right." —*April, age 12*

"Respond with respect." —*Abby, age 12*

"You have two choices...react or resolve." —*Zack, age 12*

"It is important to think." —*Quentin, age 12*

"Words have power. Choose them carefully!" —*Danielle, age 12*

"If we all work together, we are more powerful than one." —*Casey, age 12*

"Truth is the greatest gift of all." —*Sarah, age 12*

"Anything is possible!" —*April, age 12*

"I am responsible for doing the work I need to do today even though it may be very hard." —*Helen Keller*

"You're a winner when you work as hard in school as NBA players do on the court. Stay in school. It's your best move!" —*Patrick Ewing*

"Always give a 100% effort in anything that you do whether it's in sports or in school. That's all anybody can ask of you. But if you don't, then you're only cheating yourself." —*Horace Grant.*

Treat the earth well. It was not given to you by your parents. It was loaned to your by your children. —*Ancient proverb*

"Everyone living together in peace and harmony and love—is the goal we all should seek." —*Rosa Parks*

Don't be afraid to take risks. If you aren't willing to take risks, you won't ever fail. But you won't ever succeed.

"You are what you are today because of the choices you made yesterday."
—*Stephen Covey*

"Without good manners, human society becomes intolerable and impossible."
—*George Bernard Shaw*

"Few things in the world are more powerful than a positive push. A smile. A word of optimism and hope. A 'You can do it' when things are tough."

—Richard M. DeVos

"Integrity is the value we place on ourselves. It is a fundamental part of the character ethic."

—Stephen Covey

Follow your dream. Don't give up, no matter what. You may not achieve all that you dream of, but a portion of a dream is a dream come true.

"Each one of us has unique gifts or talents. And, most of our lives will be easier and happier if we make the most of those. Also, don't worry so much about what others think of you. Do what you think is right, and you'll be just fine!"

—Judy Woodruff

"The difference between mediocrity and excellence is hard work, perseverance, and good character."

—Deb Austin Brown

"The only way to be happy is to be good."

—Aristotle

"Let deeds match words."

—Plato

"Even the woodpecker owes his success to the fact that he uses his head and keeps pecking away until he finishes the job he has started."   —Coleman Cox

"You may have to fight a battle more than once to win it."   —Margaret Thatcher

"Our self-confidence is built in direct proportion to the strength and structure of our character."

—Deb Austin Brown

"Find another way."

—Satchel Paige

"Nothing is interesting if you're not interested."

—Helen Macinness

"Remember in our complex technological lives, that the most important element in teaching is still the human element."

—Deb Austin Brown

"Learning about good character helps you try harder than ever to reach your goal of earning a spot on the A Honor Roll. Then you feel good about yourself that you can achieve excellence!"

—Samara, age 11

"When you break a pillar of character, you hurt everyone."   —Cody, age 6

"Are you an architect and builder of human potential, or are you part of the demolition crew?"

—Deb Austin Brown

"How we treat one another matters."   —Barbara Walters (Charleston, WV)

"It is not important to be the best. Just do your best."   —Corey, age 12

"Our ultimate responsibility and joy come out of our willingness to contribute to the greater good."

—Carol Orsborn

"Be patient. Rome wasn't built in a day, and learning about a subject will take longer than a day as well." —Chris, age 12

There has never been an undisciplined person who was a champion.

Where you start is not as important as where you finish.

"It is better to do a good job than to talk about it. We should always do our best." —Benjamin Franklin

Today be aware of how you are spending your 1,440 beautiful minutes. Spend them wisely!

The best way to get something done is to begin.

"Thinking positively and optimistically will not only make you happier, it will make you healthier." —Michael A. Mitchell

"Adversity causes some men to break, others to break records." —William A. Ward

"Keep away from people who belittle your ambitions. Small people always do that, but the really great make you feel that you, too, can become great." —Mark Twain

"Decide what you think is right, and stick to it." —George Eliott

"If you don't know where you are going, how can you expect to get there?" —Basil S. Walsh

"To succeed in school, you have to work hard and stay on task." —Chris, age 12

"Be dedicated...to be educated." —James, age 11

It takes teamwork to make the dream work.

"If you can dream it, you can do it." —Walt Disney

Give a man a fish, and he eats for a day. Teach a man to fish, and he eats for a lifetime.

"Look for the best in others...and in yourself!" —Deb Austin Brown

Erasers are for people who are willing to correct their mistakes.

Following the path of least resistance makes rivers and men crooked.

"The world is in need today of men and women of character who will do something about wrong conditions." —Dr. Martin Luther King, Jr.

"Let us make one point—that we meet each other with a smile—even when it is difficult to smile."
—*Mother Teresa*

It does matter who started it.

A life without cause is a life without effect.

Nobody can pedal the bike for you.

Climbing the hill is more fun than standing on the top.

Whining and crying gets you more attention, but not more friends.

A tiny hole can empty a great big bucket.

Jump at the chance!

Seek out the good in people.

"He who conquers others is strong; he who conquers himself is mighty."
—*Lao-Tzu*

"Virtue is harder to be got than knowledge of the world; and, if lost in a young man, is seldom recovered."
—*John Locke*

"Allow more study time for those subjects in need of improvement."
—*Chris, age 12*

Open your arms to change, but don't let go of your values.

Remember that silence is sometimes the best answer.

Live a good, honorable life. Then when you get older and think back, you'll be able to enjoy it a second time.

Follow the 3 Rs: respect for yourself, respect for others, responsibility for your actions.

"Everest for me, and I believe the rest of the world, is the physical and symbolic manifestation of overcoming odds to achieve a dream."
—*Tom Whittaker*

"Behavior...is a mirror, in which everyone shows his image."   —*Goethe*

"Life requires thorough preparation. Veneer isn't worth anything."
—*George Washington Carver*

"Try not to become a man of success, but rather a man of value."
—*Albert Einstein*

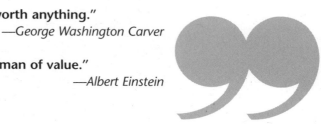

"At some time in your life, you probably had someone believe in you when you didn't believe in yourself. They scripted you. Did that make a difference in your life? What if you were a positive scripter, an affirmer, of other people?"

—*Covey desk calendar*

"Integrity is doing the right thing even when no one is watching."

—*Jim Stovall*

"I care not about what others think of what I do, but I care very much about what I think of what I do. That is character!" —*Theodore Roosevelt*

"Character, the willingness to accept responsibility for one's own life—is the source from which self-respect springs." —*Joan Didion*

"You can't have the fruits without the roots." —*Stephen Covey*

"Happiness is not a state to be arrived at—but a manner of traveling."

—*Margaret Lee Runbeck*

"All television is educational television. The question is: What is it teaching?"

—*Nicholas Johnson*

Speed is not everything. Try some direction.

"The harder the conflict, the more glorious the triumph." —*Thomas Paine*

"The good news is that the bad news can be turned into good news when you change your attitude!" —*Robert Schuller*

"A man's manners are a mirror in which he shows his portrait."

—*Johann Wolfgang von Goethe*

"Manners are of more importance than laws. Upon them, in great measure, the laws depend." —*Edmund Burke*

We are all born with a positive mental attitude. We learn to be negative.

With a good attitude, we can turn negative experiences into positive lessons.

"Dreams and dedication are a powerful combination." —*William Longgood*

"Goals are the steps on the way to your dreams." —*Casey Fitz Randolph*

If you want to see the view, first you have to climb the mountain.

In the confrontation between the stream and the rock, the stream always wins...not through strength, but through persistence.

If it is to be, it's up to me!

What you are becoming is often as important as what you are accomplishing.

Life is like a ten-speed bike. Most of us have gears we never use.

"What the best and wisest parent wants for his own child, that must the community want for all of its children." —John Dewey

If you don't take pride in who you are, you can never take pride in what you do.

The only people you should try to get even with are those who have helped you.

Love more...judge less.

The right angle to approach a difficult problem is the TRY-angle!

Anyone can be average. Is that all you want to be?

"We often live as if our habits do not matter. They do." —John Farguder

Go the extra mile!

"Ability is what you're capable of doing. Motivation determines what you do. Attitude determines how well you do it." —Lou Holtz

"Excellence is not an act but a habit. The things you do the most are the things you will do best." —Marva Collins

"If we were supposed to talk more than we listen, we would have two mouths and one ear." —Mark Twain

"We become just by the practice of just actions, self-controlled by exercising self-control, and courageous by performing acts of courage." —Aristotle

"Never take the easy way out." —Aaron Craver

"My father always taught me to give an honest day's work if I expected an honest day's pay. Today's kids need to apply that principle whether it be in regards to cutting lawns or just living life." —Joe Dumars

"Keep your word and value your reputation—it's the one thing that, once you lose it—you can't get it back." —Leeza Gibbons

"As our habits go, so goes our character." —Michael A. Mitchell

What is down in your well comes up in your bucket.

"Character is the real foundation of all worthwhile success." —John Hays Hammond

"No legacy is so rich as honesty." —William Shakespeare

"Character is higher than intellect." —Ralph Waldo Emerson

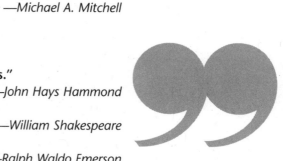

Truth is the foundation of all knowledge and the cement of all societies.

The more you stretch the truth, the more you are able to see through it.

"Honesty is the first chapter in the book of wisdom."   —Thomas Jefferson

A lie may take care of the present, but it has no future.

Honesty in little things is no little thing.

Honesty is always the best policy!

The biggest step you take is the one you take when you meet the other person halfway.

The best way to get the last word is to apologize.

"An empty bag cannot stand upright."   —Benjamin Franklin

"Coming together is a beginning; keeping together is progress; working together is success."   —Henry Ford

When one helps another, both are strong.   —German proverb

"Anytime you see a turtle up on top of a fence post, you know he had some help."   —Alex Haley

A good thing to remember and a better thing to do—work with the construction gang and not the wrecking crew!

"You cannot shake hands with a clenched fist."   —Indira Gandhi

"Help thy brother's boat across, and lo! thine own has reached the shore."   —Hindu proverb

"The price of greatness is responsibility."   —Winston Churchill

No farmer has ever plowed a field by turning it over in his mind.

No snowflake in an avalanche ever feels responsible.

"Wisdom is knowing what to do next, skill is knowing how to do it; and virtue is doing it."   —David Starr Jordan

"What we need in the world is manners."   —Eleanor Roosevelt

"Initiative is doing the right thing without being told."   —Victor Hugo

"Always do your best. What you plant now, you will harvest later."   —Og Mandino

"Let everyone sweep in front of his own door, and the whole world will be clean."
—*Goethe*

"The price of success is really much lower than the price of failure."
—*Zig Ziglar*

"Hold yourself responsible for a higher standard than anybody else expects of you. Never excuse yourself."
—*Henry Ward Beecher*

"Whenever you are to do a thing, though it can never be known but to yourself, ask yourself how you would act were all the world looking at you, and act accordingly."
—*Thomas Jefferson*

"There is no substitute for hard work."
—*Thomas Edison*

"Learning is not attained by chance...it must be sought with ardor and attended to with diligence."
—*Abigail Adams*

"The quality of a person's life is in direct proportion to their commitment to excellence, regardless of their chosen field of endeavor."
—*Vince Lombardi*

"When you are through changing, you're through."
—*Bruce Barton*

"People with goals succeed because they know where they are going."
—*Earl Nightingale*

"I think and think for months and years. Ninety-nine times, the conclusion is false. The hundredth time I am right."
—*Albert Einstein*

"Live your life as an exclamation, not an explanation."
—*H. Jackson Brown, Jr.*

"Success seems to be largely a matter of hanging on after others have let go."
—*William Feather*

"Be careful to keep your promise."
—*George Washington*

"Never use the word impossible seriously again. Toss it into the verbal wastebasket."
—*Norman Vincent Peale*

"Watch for problems. They disguise the big opportunities."
—*H. Jackson Brown, Jr.*

In life, as in golf, it is the follow-through that makes all the difference.

"The next mile is the only one a person really has to make."
—*Eric Sevareid*

"The habit of persistence is the habit of victory."
—*Herbert Kaufman*

"Great works are performed not by strength, but by perseverance."
—*Samuel Johnson*

"The impossible just takes a little longer to accomplish."
—*Wilma Rudolph*

You can get straight As and still flunk life!

"Even if you are on the right track, you will get run over if you just sit there."
—*Will Rogers*

"Progress always involves risk. You can't steal second base and keep your foot on first."
—*Frederick Wilcox*

"Be kind. For everyone you meet is fighting a hard battle."
—*Plato*

"Character may be manifested in the great moments, but it is made in the small ones."
—*Phillip Brooks*

"The good man is the man who, no matter how morally unworthy he has been, is moving to become better."
—*John Dewey*

"Weakness of attitude becomes weakness of character."
—*Albert Einstein*

"Honesty is the best policy."
—*Cervantes*

"Failure is success if we learn from it."
—*Malcolm S. Forbes*

"Character is destiny."
—*Heraclitus*

"We do not need more knowledge, we need more character."
—*John Calvin Coolidge*

"Success is always temporary. When all is said and done, the only thing you'll have left is your character."
—*Vince Gill*

"We are where we are, as we are, because of what we are."
—*Earle J. Glade*

"Character develops itself in the stream of life."
—*Johann Wolfgang von Goethe*

"In matters of style, swim with the current. In matters of principle, stand like a rock."
—*Thomas Jefferson*

"Giving thanks is a course from which we never graduate."
—*Valerie Anders*

"You will never find time for anything. You must make it."
—*Charles Buxton*

"Character cannot be developed in ease and quiet. Only through experiences of trial and suffering can the soul be strengthened, vision cleared, ambition inspired, and success achieved."
—*Helen Keller*

"I am a teacher. A teacher is someone who leads. There is no magic here. I do not walk on water, I do not part the sea. I just love the children."
—*Marva Collins*

"The true measure of a man is how he treats someone who can do him absolutely no good."
—*Ann Landers*

"One man with courage makes a majority."
—Andrew Jackson

"Do unto others as you would have them do unto you."
—The Golden Rule

"Character is the result of two things: mental attitude and the way we spend our time."
—Elbert Hubbard

"What lies behind us and what lies before us are small matters compared to what lies within us."
—Oliver Wendell Holmes

"The true test of character is not how much we know how to do, but how we behave when we don't know what to do."
—Jon Holt

"Actions, looks, words, and steps form the alphabet by which you may spell character."
—Johann Kaspar Lavater

" What you see and hear depends a great deal on where you are standing; it also depends on what sort of person you are."
—C.S. Lewis

"Things turn out best for the people who make the best of the way things turn out."
—Art Linkletter

"Energy and persistence conquer all things."
—Benjamin Franklin

"Nothing in this world can take the place of persistence."
—Calvin Coolidge

"Character is much easier kept than recovered."
—Thomas Paine

"No man can climb out beyond the limitations of his own character."
—John Lord Morley

"Live in such a way that you would not be ashamed to sell your parrot to the town gossip."
—Will Rogers

"Sow a thought, reap an act. Sow an act, reap a habit. Sow a habit, reap a character. Sow a character, reap a destiny."
—Charles Reade

"Character, in the long run, is the decisive factor in the life of an individual and of nations alike."
—Theodore Roosevelt

"When I approach a child, he inspires in me two sentiments: tenderness for what he is, and respect for what he may become."
—Louis Pasteur

"Be more concerned with your character than with your reputation. Your character is what you really are, while your reputation is merely what others think you are."
—John Wooden

Good character, like good soup, is usually homemade.

"Three things in human life are important. The first is to be kind. The second is to be kind. And, the third is to be kind."
—Henry James

"Fall seven times, stand up eight."

—*Japanese proverb*

"Life's most persistent and urgent question is this: **What are you doing for others?**"

—*Martin Luther King, Jr.*

"Kindness is the golden chain by which society is bound together."   —*Goethe*

"Look for the good in people and expect to find it."   —*William Shakespeare*

"Children need love, especially when they do not deserve it."

—*Harold S. Hubert*

"No act of kindness, no matter how small, is ever wasted."   —*Aesop*

"There is joy in transcending self to serve others."   —*Mother Teresa*

"Never give up on anybody. Miracles happen every day."—*H. Jackson Brown, Jr.*

There is a helping hand at the end of your arm.

"Never doubt that a small group of thoughtful, committed citizens can change the world; indeed, it's the only thing that ever has."   —*Margaret Meade*

"Everybody can be great because everybody can serve. Make a career of humanity and you will make a greater person of yourself, a greater nation of your country, and a finer world to live in."   —*Martin Luther King, Jr.*

"I use not only all the brains I have, but all I can borrow."   —*Woodrow Wilson*

"A bit of fragrance always clings to the hand that gives roses."

—*Chinese proverb*

Whenever you find a dream inside your heart, don't ever let it go. For dreams are the tiny seeds from which tomorrows grow!

"Winners in the game of life have an attitude of gratitude!"

—*Coach Jayson Gee*

"If we are to reach real peace in the world, we shall have to begin with children."

—*Gandhi*

"Good character doesn't cost you a cent, but it's worth everything!"

—*Heather, age 12*

"No one ever injured his eyesight by looking on the bright side of things."

—*Helen Keller*

"You can't buy trust. You earn it."   —*Heather, age 12*

"Physical fatigue will fade in the face of a dream. Some things are worth working for!"

—*Braeden Kershner*

Attitude: The difference between winners and losers.

You have to give respect to get it!

Sometimes honesty takes real courage, but it's always the right thing to do!

"Without change, we cannot grow."   —Chad Pennington

"People need responsibility. They resist assuming it, but they cannot get along without it."   —John Steinbeck

You are judged by the company you keep...and the company you keep out of!

"Example is not the main thing in influencing others, it is the only thing."   —Albert Schweitzer

You are responsible for building your own character. No one can build it for you!

Become the most positive and enthusiastic person you know!

"Manners are the happy way of doing things."   —Ralph Waldo Emerson

"Correction does much, encouragement more."   —Johann Wolfgang von Goethe

"There can be no daily democracy without daily citizenship."   —Ralph Nader

"Even when I went to the playground, I picked the guys with less talent—but who were willing to work hard and put in the effort—who had the desire to be great."   —Earvin Magic Johnson

Dream big. Work hard!

Never deprive someone of hope. It might be all he has.

The best thing to wear is a smile!

"I will be sure...always."   —Motto for the United States Air National Guard

Ability may get you to the top, but it takes character to keep you there.

Never look down on anyone unless you are helping them up.

Lighthouses don't blow horns. They just shine!

"In a world where there is so much to be done, I felt strongly impressed that there must be something for me to do."   —Dorothea Dix

Knowing what you stand for limits what you will fall for.

It's easy to sit up and take notice. What's difficult is standing up and taking action.

The biggest risk you take is the one you don't take.

The trouble with letting off steam is it gets you into more hot water.

When looking for faults—use a mirror, not a telescope!

"Small things done with great love bring joy and peace."　　　—Mother Teresa

"The world is a dangerous place to live in. Not because people do evil, but because people sit by and let them."　　　—Albert Einstein

Success depends more on your backbone than on your wishbone.

Be reliable! Earning the trust of another is a valuable thing.

Success comes in cans. I can! You can! We can!

If a task is once begun, never leave it 'til it's done. Be the labor great or small, do it well or not at all!

"We are here to help one another along life's journey."　　　—William Bennett

"There is no greater loan than a sympathetic ear."　　　—Frank Tyger

"Freedom is the right to be wrong, not the right to do wrong."　　　—John G. Diefenbaker

"When we turn to each other, and not on each other, that's victory."　　　—Jesse Jackson

"Be not simply good, be good for something."　　　—Henry David Thoreau

"Write injuries in sand, kindness in marble."　　　—French proverb

"Alone we can do so little; together, we can do so much."　　　—Helen Keller

"Fighting doesn't prove anything. Real strength comes from the heart."　　　—Sam, age 8

"I never learn anything from talking. I only learn when I ask questions."　　　—Lou Holtz

Today's mighty oak is just yesterday's nut that held its ground.

"The best time to plant a tree was twenty years ago. The second best time is now."　　　—Chinese proverb

Character is contagious. Is yours worth catching?

"The childhood shows the man, as morning shows the day."   —John Milton

"It is common sense to take a method and try it. If it fails, admit it frankly and try another. But above all, try something."   —Franklin D. Roosevelt

Those who are good at making excuses are seldom good at making anything else.

Kindness is difficult to give away because it keeps coming back.

Nothing ruins the truth like stretching it.

Wisdom has two parts: having a lot to say—and not saying it.

Worry is the darkroom in which negatives are developed.

"Live the truth instead of professing it."   —Elbert Hubbard

"If you tell the truth, you don't have to remember anything."   —Mark Twain

Children spell love...T-I-M-E.

The best way to teach character is to have it around the house.

"If it is desirable that children be kind, appreciative, and pleasant—then those qualities should be taught—not hoped for."   —James Dobson

"An optimist is a guy that figures when the soles of his shoes wear out, that he is just back on his feet again!"   —Zig Ziglar

You can complain because rose bushes have thorns, or you can rejoice because thorn bushes have roses.

"Go as far as you can see, and when you get there you will always be able to see further."   —Zig Ziglar

"There can be no happiness for people at the expense of other people."   —Anwar el-Sadat

"Invest in a human soul. Who knows? It might be a diamond in the rough."   —Mary McLeod Bethune

"Determination and perseverance move the world; thinking that others will do it for you is a sure way to fail."   —Marva Collins

"Before we even attempt to teach children, we want them to know each of them is unique and very special. We want them to like themselves, to want to achieve and care about themselves."   —Marva Collins

"Genuine success does not come from proclaiming our values, but from consistently putting them into daily action."　　　　—Ken Blanchard

"A wise man will make more opportunities than he finds."　　　—Francis Bacon

"Hard work is good for us!"　　　　　　　　　　　　　　　—Hal Urban

"Hard work never hurt anyone."　　　　　　　　　　　　—Maw Great

"There are no shortcuts to any place worth going."　　　　—Beverly Sills

"When you expect the best, you release a magnetic force in your mind which—by the law of attraction—tends to bring the best to you."
　　　　　　　　　　　　　　　　　　　　　—Norman Vincent Peale

"There can be no happiness if the things we believe in are different from the things that we do."　　　　　　　　　　　　　　　—Freya Stark

"As soon as you trust yourself, you will know how to live."　　—Goethe

What The Kids Say...

Dear Ms. Brown,

Thank you for teaching me good character. I will miss you the most of all. You have always been nice to me. You always gave me a second chance. Just like when I didn't have a backboard for my science fair project. You patted me on the back and said that everything's going to be all right and not to worry about it. I got a good grade on it, and I'm proud of my work. I think that you are the nicest teacher, friend, and parent to me.

Love, Danielle

Dear Ms. Brown,

When we first came here we didn't know anything about The Golden Rule. When you taught us about character, every time I do something I feel bad about it.

Love, Quentin

Dear Ms. Brown,

I learned a lot about character at Weimer Elementary School. I am very glad that the teachers here at Weimer teach character. When I came in this classroom I had no idea what to do when you said "character." Then I started to panic because I didn't know what to do, but now I know a lot about character. A character sentence is something like this: Don't do what's easy, do what's right!

Love, Chris

Dear Ms. Brown,

You have been the best teacher ever in the whole universe. You are funny, nice, and fun. You have taught us more than enough. You have not only taught us school work, but you have taught us so much about character and how to be a good person. When we had doubts, you gave us motivation. You not only tell us about character, you live it and set an example. Character is very important in life, and I am so thankful that you were there to show us everything there is to know. Now that I know about character I can live it and be a better person. You taught us character also helps you in your school work. You have helped us when we had conflicts, you helped us make up. You not only do your job, you go beyond. You have been a good friend this year. Thanks again for everything. YOU ARE MY HERO.

Love, Casey

Dear Ms. Brown,

On the first day of school I was new, and I had no idea about character. Every time you said something about it, I was puzzled. When you asked what The Golden Rule meant, only one person knew what it was. But now everyone knows what it means, which is to treat everyone the way you want to be treated. I would have been happy last year to know it. If I knew The Golden Rule, I would have taught it to my brother because he was bad. But now that he has met you, he has really straightened up. It really helps kids!

Love, Barbara

Dear Sixth Grade Students of 1999-2000,

My name is Crystal, and I went to Weimer for eight years. Now I am in junior high. I want to say that I hope you will respect the teachers and every other person. Ms. Brown is a very loving and caring teacher with a good heart. I respected her for who and what she is.

I went from Es in every grade until I got on the B Honor Roll in sixth grade. I hope you all will do well in school. As Ms. Brown would say, "Always try your best!" I did, and I passed! The only person who thought I could do it was Ms. Brown, and I want to thank her for that. Thank you, Ms. Brown!

Love, Crystal

Mrs. Brown,

I wanted to give you something before you left our school. It's something really special. I want for you to promise me that you will take these two pennies wherever you go when you go places to tell them about good character. The dates on the pennies are really important. 1991 is the year I was born, and 1997 is the year that I was in your class. That's the year that my life was changed—learning about character!

I wish you wouldn't have to go. I will miss you.

Love, Will

Ms. Brown,

You are the best teacher I ever had because of character. Character is cool, and I follow the Golden Rule.

Thanks, Holden

Dear Ms. Brown,

When I first came here, I didn't know what the Golden Rule was. I'm glad you taught it to me!

Love, Sarah L.

Dear Mrs. Brown,

Thank you for teaching me good character. It will go on forever and ever!

Love, Sarah G.

Hi, Mrs. Brown!

I have been doing a lot better in my school work this year in junior high. I don't have the A or B Honor Roll yet, but I am close to it. I still remember what we all learned about character last year. I miss you!

Love, Karen

To: Mrs. Brown,

We will always miss you so much. You gave us the key to believe in ourselves. You stood up for us in good times and in bad. You always have a smile on your face, and you never got mad. So, wherever you go—one mile or ten—you will never leave our hearts. Please teach the Character Class wherever you go!

Love, Josh

Dear Mrs. Brown,

I will miss having the character classes. But I hope you teach it at another school. I will miss running into you in the halls and talking about character and life. I'll just miss being in the character class next year, and I'll just miss talking to you.

Love, Andrew

Mrs. Brown,

I learned a lot this year about character. I learned a lot about the Golden Rule. I will probably teach it to my kids and they will teach it to their kids, and it will go on forever. I have learned a lot from you. You have been like a mom to me. If you get my sister in class next year, I hope you give her some character lessons and lectures.

Love, April

Dear Ms. Brown,

I learned a lot from all of the character lessons this year. I came in one person and went out another. I have learned that there is no reason to have bad character. I will try my best to carry on what I have learned this year for the rest of my life. Thanks for teaching me character. All the lessons and lectures help.

Love, Danielle

As We Were Going To Press...

[As this book was going to press, the story of Cody and his father came full circle. The story has such a powerful ending, that we wanted to include it here.]

As you may remember, Cody and I were together my last year of teaching at Lakewood Elementary School. He was in the class I wrote about in Chapter One of this book. Like all of my classes over the years, these kids were special. I will never forget them.

I left Lakewood five years ago and found a job across town at Weimer Elementary. Little could I imagine that four years later, Cody would follow me there. I was so surprised when I found out that he was in the fourth grade class, just down the hall from me. It was wonderful seeing him there! I put my arm around him and said, "Cody, it simply could *not* be a coincidence that you and I are both here at Weimer. We are both character messengers, and I think we both have important work to do." Cody just grinned.

About three months later, Cody met me outside near the bus at the end of the day. He came running towards me with that signature smile of his. I could tell that he had good news to share. "Dad is up for parole soon, and he may be getting out of prison early for good behavior!" Cody announced. We looked at each other in that familiar, understanding way. We didn't need words to communicate the importance of this wonderful event. The look in our eyes said it all.

About nine weeks after that, I was coming back into the school building after walking my students to the bus. Down the long hallway, I saw Cody and a man walking towards me. As they got closer, I knew this must be his dad. The three of us broke into a smile. I extended my hand and said, "You must be Cody's dad. I am so happy to meet you! I am Deb Brown, his former kindergarten teacher."

"I know who you are," said Cody's father. "You are the teacher who changed my life."

"Changed *your* life?" I questioned.

"You changed Cody, and he changed me," instructed this paroled convict.

"But it was never me," I corrected. "It was the message...the character message!"

Cody stood there, looking up and grinning, as his father and I talked. He told me how Cody had continued to send him character quotes in prison, even after I had left Lakewood. He said that Cody impressed upon him the importance of getting a good education, so he had enrolled in adult education classes while in prison—earning his high school equivalency diploma. He seemed determined to be a better citizen and a better role model for his son.

At the end of our talk, Cody's dad shook my hand again and said his thanks. I humbly accepted his gratitude, but told him that the real thanks belong to *him*— for taking the time and making the effort to come and talk with me so all of us would know the ending to this story. So all of us would know the real power of the character message in changing the lives of *real* people, who in turn, go out into the world to change the lives of others.

I am happy to say that the character message is alive and well in Cody's home. God bless Cody and his dad—as they embark on a promising future. And God bless us all, as we go out into the world carrying the character message to every student we meet!

Afterword

So *you're* interested in taking your own students on the character journey? It is my hope that this book has inspired and motivated you and moved you to action. I'll be along the road cheering you onward. Travel tips? Mine are simply this: Tune in to kids, create an awareness, and look for life's natural wisdom to create meaningful lessons in character for your kids. Cultivating the *character climate* is the most important step! When you love your students enough to weave the character message into *all* that you do, you are well on your way. By rolling up your shirtsleeves and trying things yourself, you will learn what you need to do for your students.

> You'll learn more about a road by traveling it than by consulting all of the maps in the world.

Each year will be different. Remember to be on the lookout for road signs along the way. The idea to teach character lessons during detention time grew into a school-wide character class. And, out of that class, grew our staff's commitment to form a character team. In your journey with kids, plant plenty of seeds along the way and be a patient gardener. The harvest will be bountiful!

Along the way, take time for an occasional glance in your rearview mirror. You will see just how far you've traveled. And when you are tired, seeing your progress will serve as the needed fuel to propel you onward. Keep records and journals of your work with kids. They will serve as powerful documentation of your journey! To make it simple, I keep a three-ring binder nearby. Whenever I witness evidence of character taking root within my classroom, I write myself a note. Whenever I see written evidence in a child's artwork or journal or written assignments, I simply ask the student for permission to make a copy for my notebook. Students always agree! In fact, they love to look through the notebook and are often proud of all the wonderful ways we have grown in character.

The journey is not always easy. There are times when you will feel frustrated and overwhelmed. I understand. I've been there. For ten years my classroom was an island of character education within my school. We were the only class intentionally teaching, learning, and trying to live out the character message. But as you have read in this book, we became *the little classroom that could!* We spread the message! With lots of hard work on the part of students and teachers, we became the little school that grew in character. It can happen for you, too. The fact that you are reading this book means you have already begun your travels. There is a wonderful and exciting road ahead. I wish you and your students a successful journey!

About the Author

Deb Brown is a teacher by heart. She has been honored with several teaching awards, including the Milken Family Foundation National Educator Award and the Ashland Oil Teacher Achievement Award. Her work extends beyond the classroom to include speaking about her books and character development at education conferences, schools, and businesses across America. She has carried the character message to parents, students, educators, and business leaders from thirty-three states.

Deb is the author of *Lessons From The Rocking Chair: Timeless Stories For Teaching Character* and *Lessons From The Beach Chair: Nature's Wisdom For Teaching Character*. She spends her free time writing, beach combing and watching the night sky. Deb lives in her hometown of St. Albans, West Virginia, but spends her summers in Garden City Beach, South Carolina. She is the proud mother of two grown sons, Aaron and Ben. Recently Deb was blessed with her first grandchild, Meg. Now, more than ever, Deb feels called to carry the character message out into the world.